Lighthouses of England
The South West

The lighthouses of Cornwall, North Devon, Somerset and the Bristol Channel

Tony Denton and Nicholas Leach

▲ Trevose Head lighthouse near Padstow.

◀ (frontispiece) Godrevy Island with its lighthouse on Cornwall's north coast.

▶ (opposite) Round Island lighthouse in the Isles of Scilly.

◀◀ (front cover) Lundy North lighthouse.

Published by
Foxglove Publishing Ltd
Foxglove House
Shute Hill
Lichfield
Staffordshire WS13 8DB
England
Tel (07940) 905046
www.foxglovepublishing.co.uk

© Nicholas Leach and Tony Denton 2011, revised 2018

The rights of Tony Denton and Nicholas Leach to be identified as the Authors of this work have been asserted in accordance with the Copyrights, Designs and Patents Act 1988.
All rights reserved. No part of this book may be reprinted or reproduced or utilised in any form or by any electronic, mechanical or other means, now known or hereafter invented, including photocopying and recording, or in any information storage or retrieval system, without permission in writing from the publishers.

British Library Cataloguing in Publication Data. A catalogue record for this book is available from the British Library.

ISBN 978-0-9564560-3-8

Layout and design by Nicholas Leach

Printed in Great Britain

Contents

Lighthouse History   4

South East England Lighthouses   13
Looe 14, Polperro 15, Fowey 16, Mevagissey 18, St Anthony's 20, Lizard 22, Penzance 26, Newlyn 27, Tater Du 28, Longships 30, Wolf Rock 34, Peninnis, Scilly 38, Round Island, Scilly 40, St Agnes, Scilly 42, Bishop Rock, Scilly 44, Pendeen 46, St Ives 48, Hayle 50, Portreath 51, Godrevy Island 52, Trevose Head 54, Hartland Point 58, River Tawe 60, Bull Point 64, Lundy 68, Ilfracombe 72, Lynmouth Foreland 74, Watchet 76, Burnham-on-Sea 78, Blacknore Point 82, Portishead Point 84, Avonmouth 86, River Severn 88

Glossary   94

Appendix   95
Bibliography, Websites, Acknowledgements

Index   96

Lighthouse History

1538 Reputed to be Cornwall's earliest light on St Nicholas Chapel, St Ives

1680 The first lighthouse on Isles of Scilly at St Agnes

1691 Coal fired light at Lizard

1752 Twin lights built at Lizard Point

1794 First attempt to mark Land's End with beacon on Longships

1795 First beacon erected on Wolf Rock

1820 Four lighthouses built to mark river Tawe at Braunton and Instow

1820 First lighthouse built on Lundy Island

1847 First lighthouse on Cornwall's north coast at Trevose Head

1858 Lighthouse built on Bishop Rock

1859 The only off shore lighthouse on Cornwall's north coast at Godrevy

1870 First lighthouse on Wolf Rock

1965 The most recent Cornish lighthouse built at Tater Du

1972 Bull Point lighthouse partly destroyed by cliff fall

1973 Trinity House's first helipad erected on Wolf Rock

1974 Latest Devon lighthouse built at Bull Point to replace temporary light

2009 Heritage centre opened at Lizard Point

This book provides a comprehensive guide to the aids to navigation, lighthouses and harbour lights around the coasts of south-west England, including Cornwall, the Isles of Scilly, North Devon, Somerset and the Bristol Channel. It starts at the Devon/Cornwall border and ends with the small but numerous lights along the river Severn. This area has some of the more famous and historically significant lighthouses in the British Isles, with the Lizard, Longships and Wolf Rock towers being particularly well known.

While the Corporation of Trinity House is responsible for many of these lights, including all the major ones, a number of significant small harbour lights are also in operation, such as at Mevagissey, Fowey and Penzance, and details of these aids to navigation are also included.

This introduction is intended to provide an overview of lighthouse history, development and organisation in England and Wales, focussing on the need for lights to mark the coasts of Cornwall, Devon and the Bristol Channel, and explaining how Trinity House has developed into the service it is today.

The first lights

Many vessels have been wrecked on the coast of Cornwall, which has a reputation for being one of the most treacherous in Britain, as well as in the Bristol Channel with its strong tidal currents and shallow waters. Many and various dangers have to be negotiated by the mariner who is either navigating past the West Country to other destinations, or intending to enter one of the region's ports or harbours.

Along Cornwall's south coast are many inlets, estuaries and natural harbours, which can safely accommodate vessels both small and large, but whose entrances can catch out the unwary. The north coast, on the other hand, is characterised by rugged cliffs and rocks which take the full force of the Atlantic in the prevailing westerly wind. And the Bristol Channel is notable for having one of the biggest tidal ranges in the world, with the strong currents likely to cause confusion for navigators.

As trading by sea has been a principal activity of all civilisations, ensuring the safety of goods and cargoes moved by water is of paramount importance. Navigating by sea involves facing difficulties and dangers such as storms and bad weather, avoiding reefs, headlands, sandbanks and cliffs, and making safe passage into ports and harbours. The need for aids to navigation is therefore as old as trading by sea itself.

The earliest aids to navigation were beacons or daymarks, sited near harbours or ports rather than on headlands or reefs, to help ships reach their destination safely. The earliest lighthouses were in the Mediterranean and the oldest such structure of which records survive was that on the island of Pharos, off Alexandra, on the northern coast of Egypt. The Pharos lighthouse, 466ft tall, was built between 283BC and 247BC and survived until 1326.

The first navigational lights guarding the coasts of the West Country were probably ecclesiastical ones, displayed from medieval coastal churches. One of these was shown from St Michael's Mount near Penzance, where a unique lighthouse cresset was built on the top of the fourteenth century tower of the church. Erected at the southwest corner of the crenellated parapet, it was intended to guide ships into the small harbour, which was an important tin exporting port at the time. Exact details of its usage and how long it survived are unknown.

Another medieval lighthouse in the West Country is that at Ilfracombe, which was shown from a chapel dedicated to St Nicholas that stands on Lantern Hill overlooking the entrance to the harbour. Again, exact details of its origin and operation are unknown, but the light is still

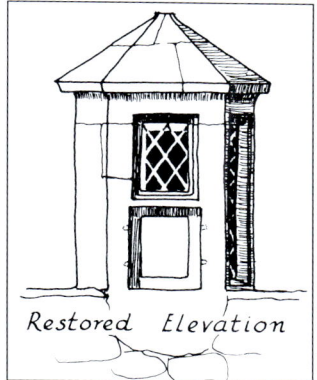

◀ Line drawing of the stone lantern cresset mounted on the top of the church tower on St Michael's Mount to house an oil lamp dating from the fifteenth century.

▲ St Michael's Mount on Cornwall's south coast no longer shows any aid to navigation.

◀ The lighthouse shown from the medieval St Nicholas Chapel in Ilfracombe, seen from the north elevation.

Lighthouse History

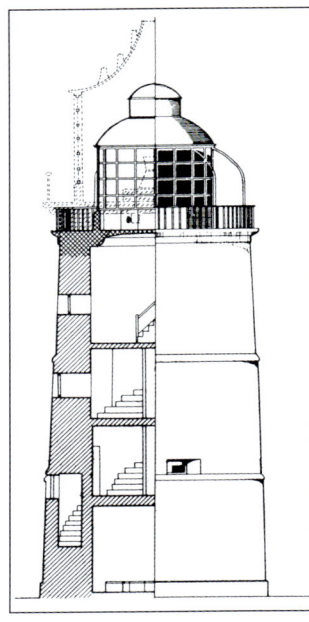

▶ Diagram of the lighthouse at St Agnes dates from 1680 with some additions made in the early nineteenth century.

displayed and the building, as well as the hill on which it stands, is one of the town's landmarks.

As well as the ecclesiastical lights, privately-built and funded lighthouses were erected at various locations before the industrial revolution took hold in Britain. One such light was that built at Burnham on Sea in Somerset where, in 1800, a number of masters and shipowners prevailed upon the Rev David Davies, the curate, to erect a lighthouse on the understanding that they would contribute voluntarily to its support. This agreement worked well for a number of years, but in 1813 he had to appeal to Trinity House to obtain a grant from government for increased and

▶ The Lizard lighthouse showing its lanterns from 1752, circa 1813 and 1904. The tower on the left is the first one, with subsequent improvements. The tower was electrified in 1924 and today shows a light with a range of twenty-six nautical miles.

▲ The lighthouse at Godrevy, completed in 1859, guards the north coast of Cornwall.

obligatory dues as he found that the income of about £135 a year he received from the mariners did not enable him to maintain the lighthouse effectively.

A lease was granted for 100 years allowing the curate to collect three shillings from coasting vessels and five shillings from foreign vessels, thus enabling him to improve the light, but by 1834 he was again running at a loss. Consequently, when Trinity House offered £13,682 for the eighty-five remaining years of the lease he soon accepted it.

The first two lighthouses to be built in Cornwall were at Lizard and St Agnes, Isles of Scilly. The Lizard lighthouse was established in 1619 by Sir John Killigrew, or Arwenack, who obtained a patent from James I in 1619. He then faced fierce opposition from local inhabitants, who benefited from looting wrecked ships and feared the light would reduce this source of income. Nevertheless, the tower was built and the fire lit, but it lasted for at most three years as shipowners were reluctant to pay light dues for its upkeep. Killigrew relied on voluntary contributions which, perhaps not surprisingly, were not forthcoming.

More than a century passed before another light was erected at the Lizard, with a

▼ An aerial view of the twin towers at Lizard, with the keepers' cottages.

Lighthouse History

▲ The impressive station at Hartland was established in 1874 with a large accommodation block for the keepers.

▼ The famous Longships lighthouse off Land's End, pictured after the addition of the helipad.

patent issued in 1756 for two lighthouses to be built by Trinity House. The Corporation, however, did not get involved in this light and leased their rights for sixty-one years at an annual rate of £80 to Thomas Fonnerau.

At St Agnes the Corporation was involved from the outset and the tower of 1680 was among the first lighthouses to be built by Trinity House. The coal fire was burned in a large fire basket in a completely enclosed lantern that was constructed of wood, covered externally and internally with lead. This was one of the first fully-enclosed coal fired lanterns and it served for more than a century before being converted to oil lamps and twenty-one reflectors in 1790.

Trinity House

The Corporation of Trinity House is the organisation responsible for the operation and maintenance of the major aids to navigation today. The exact origins of Trinity House are obscure, but probably date back to the early thirteenth century, when groups of tradesmen, such as seamen, masters of merchant vessels and pilots, formed guilds to protect their interests. One of the earliest such organisations was the Deptford Trinity House, which was incorporated by Royal Charter after its members had petitioned Henry VIII to prohibit unqualified pilots on the Thames in 1513. Deptford was then a busy port and the main point of entry for the capital's trade, so pilotage duties were lucrative, and Trinity House members wanted to retain their monopoly.

Trinity House's involvement in lighthouse construction was relatively limited until the nineteenth century, but the organisation granted leases on lighthouse to private operators, such as that at the Lizard. It was involved at some places, such as St Agnes and others on England's east coast, but it was rather slow to start building lighthouses.

Relatively few lighthouses were built prior to the nineteenth century, mainly due to financial issues as finding sufficient money to pay for lighthouse building and maintenance was problematic to say the least. However, following a series of reforms in the nineteenth century, notably an Act of Parliament passed in 1836 which abolished privately owned or leased lighthouses, Trinity House was able to considerably expand its operations, having become the sole body responsible for aids to navigation in England and Wales.

Lighthouses at Godrevy, Round Island, Trevose Head, Hartland Point and Bull Point were among those stations established during the era of expansion following the 1836 Act. In addition, a number of notable rock lighthouses were built by Trinity House during this era, notably Bishop Rock, Longships and Wolf Rock in the south-west, and these remain major landmarks. Building the rock lighthouses was an engineering challenge, and the difficulties to be overcome by the engineers involved in these projects were considerable.

Following the era of lighthouse expansion in the nineteenth century, during the twentieth century Trinity House embarked upon a programme of automation. Although many significant lights were not automated until the end of the century, some were never

▲ Hartland Point lighthouse today after the dwellings had been dismantled.

▼ Round Island and its lighthouse is situated just over two miles north of St Mary's on the Isles of Scilly.

▲ St Anthony's lighthouse at the entrance to Falmouth harbour was built in 1835 with the fog bell in place at the front of the tower. This was dismantled in 1954 and donated to a local church.

was Eddystone in 1982, and between then and 1998 all major lighthouses were automated and the keepers withdrawn.

Harbour lights

Around the West Country are a plethora of small, locally-operated lights of varying sizes and range, which operate mainly around ports, harbours and estuaries to ensure vessels' safety. Cornwall has many small harbours, and most have lighthouses at their entrance, while a number of beacons and daymarks can also be seen around the county.

Some, such as St Ives which dates from the eighteenth century, have significant historical towers, albeit on a smaller scale than that of the major aids to navigation. Others, such as that at Fowey from where china clay is exported, mark harbour entrances that can be difficult to negotiate but have been economically important. Many of Cornwall's small harbours were developed to handle tin mined in the county, and lighthouses

manned, such as the 1911-built Peninnis Head on Scilly, which showed an automatic light from its establishment. Godrevy was a manned station until 1934, when an acetylene light was installed. And the newest lighthouse in Cornwall, Tater Du, was also automated when built. The first of Trinity House's major lighthouses to be automated

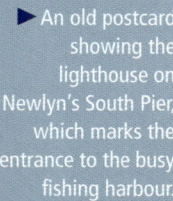

▶ An old postcard showing the lighthouse on Newlyn's South Pier, which marks the entrance to the busy fishing harbour.

Lighthouse History

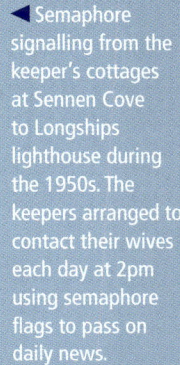

◀ Semaphore signalling from the keeper's cottages at Sennen Cove to Longships lighthouse during the 1950s. The keepers arranged to contact their wives each day at 2pm using semaphore flags to pass on daily news.

◀ For lighthouse keepers to transfer on and off rock lighthouses, such as here at Bishop Rock, required them to be winched off by a crane to a tender waiting below, and even on a calm day this could be a highly hazardous procedure.

were often built to mark their entrances. Although places such as Mevagissey, Penzance and Newlyn have miniature lighthouses, many small lights at the minor harbours are mounted on poles or walls and display a simple fixed light.

Lightkeepers

Throughout the history of lighthouses, the lightkeeper has played an essential role in maintaining the light. However, during the latter half of the twentieth century, the era of manned lighthouses came to an end as automation became the norm. Although before automation, most lights were manned, many described in this book were designed to be fully automatic from the outset.

The idealised view of lighthouse keepers conjures up a romantic image of men living in a tower with only the sea for company. While this was true for

▶ Along the coast path westwards from Fowey is Gribben Head with its well known daymark. This famous structure marks the eastern limits of St Austell Bay and the western entrance to the Fowey Estuary. Built in 1832, the 85ft square castellated stone structure has a doorway and a set of steps to the top. Painted in red and white horizontal bands it can be clearly seen for several miles. The daymark is owned by the National Trust and is on occasions open to the public.

rock stations such as Longstone and Wolf Rock, where keepers were confined to fairly cramped quarters for weeks, the reality for most keepers was different.

Most lights on the mainland, such as Trevose Head, Lizard and Pendeen, had a principal keeper, who would be supported by two assistant keepers, usually with families. The primary task of the lightkeeper was to operate and maintain the aids to navigation and ancillary equipment, and ensure that the equipment, including the reflectors and lenses, was maintained to the highest standard. With automation, the lights are now controlled from a central location, and a locally-based attendant is responsible for maintenance.

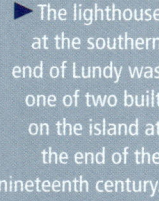

▶ The lighthouse at the southern end of Lundy was one of two built on the island at the end of the nineteenth century.

South West lighthouses

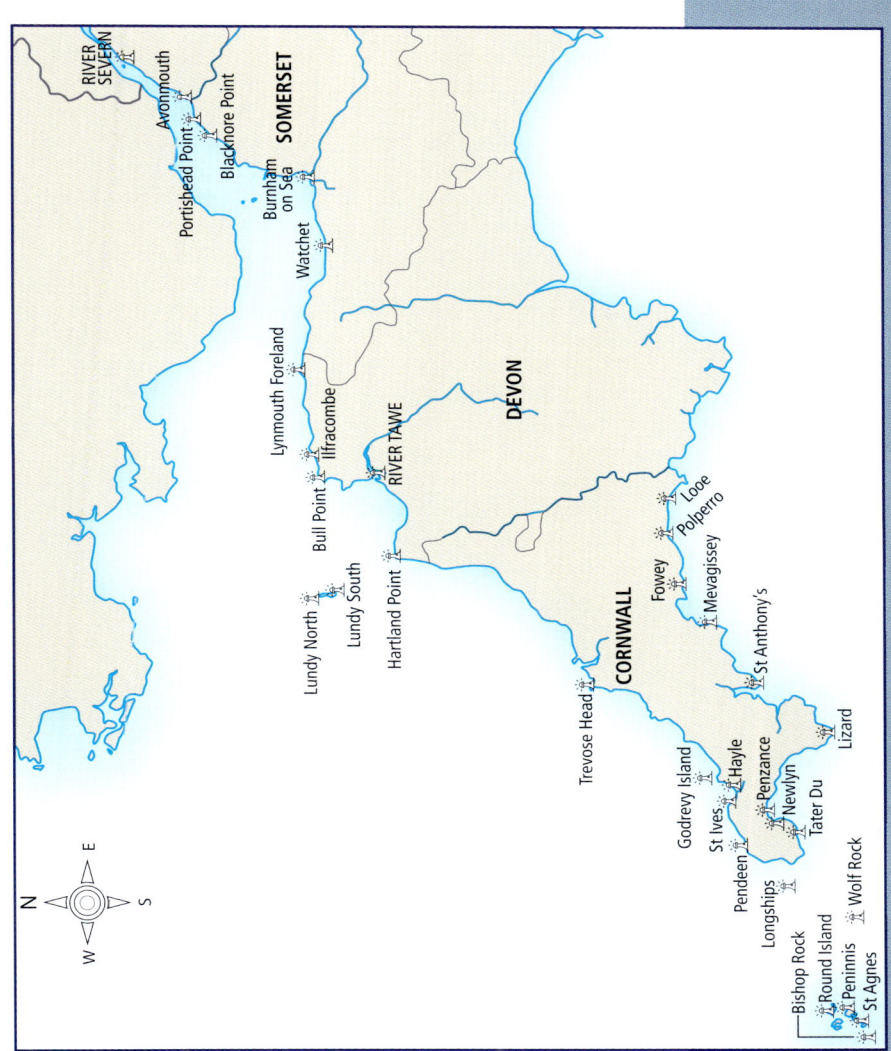

This guide to the lighthouses of the south west starts on the Devon/Cornwall border, with some small lights, then moves west to Land's End and the Isles of Scilly, before running north-east along Cornwall and Devon's north coasts, ending with the lighthouses in the Bristol Channel. The photographs show the lighthouses as they are today, and a number of historic images have also been included. The information about visiting should be used only as a starting point. Consulting road atlases and Ordnance Survey maps is advisable before planning a visit to any of the lights.

Looe

ESTABLISHED
1860

CURRENT TOWER
1860

OPERATOR
Looe Harbour Authority

ACCESS
The pier is open to the public and it is possible to walk up to the light

Although the river Looe dries out at low tide, this does not stop the town having a thriving fleet of small fishing and pleasure boats. When conditions are too dangerous to haul boats ashore, a flag is flown from a flagstaff and, in bad weather, storm signals are shown from the coastguard station.

The entrance to the river on its eastern side is channelled by the Banjo Pier, on the end of which is a 20ft red cylindrical cast-iron light with a white railed gallery. Erected in 1860, the light tower is accessed via a sloping metal ladder. A white sightboard is situated to seaward. Apart from the ladder, it is similar to the light at Whitehouse Point, Fowey. The light displays an occulting red and white light, which is visible for fifteen miles. The red sectors, visible for twelve miles, cover the Needles Eye to the west and Limmicks to the east.

The light was originally equipped with a fog signal, which gave two blasts of two seconds every thirty seconds, but water cascading over the light rendered it useless and so in 1966 it was replaced by a new signal, housed in a white 10ft square concrete pillbox, with a square opening. The horn, sounded when fishing boats are at sea, produces a three-second blast every thirty seconds.

▶ The small harbour light at the end of Looe's Banjo Pier. One of the major hazards along the coast to the east of Fowey is Looe Island and the Renny Reef which extends south-eastwards.

Polperro

ESTABLISHED	1911
CURRENT TOWER	1911
OPERATOR	Polperro Harbour Trust
ACCESS	Via the coast path east of the village for about 1,000 yards, with a short detour to the right

The village of Polperro with its tidal harbour survived for centuries on fishing and smuggling. The smuggling ceased at the end of the eighteenth century and the local economy now relies largely on tourism and a fishing fleet of small boats. With vessels needing to avoid the East Polca and Peak rocks at all tides, and the Rannys at low tide, the local harbour trust, set up in 1894, erected a lighthouse on the headland at Spy House Point in 1911.

Named after the point, this light is supported on a white 12ft high cylindrical brick tower with a doorway at the base which is now blocked up, and is mounted on a stone-paved surround with guard rails. The automatic light is contained in a small white with black trim cylindrical lantern and shows both red, to the west, and white, to the east, quick-flashing sectors visible for eight miles. The harbour is protected by one outer and two inner piers which form an 8ft opening into the inner tidal basin. The centre section has a hydraulic gate which is closed in bad weather. On the end of the western pier is a 4ft unpainted stone cylindrical pedestal which supports a squat round lantern and simple navigation light. This light, visible for four miles, flashes white when the harbour is open and red when it is closed.

◀ The small light at Spy House Point marks the entrance to the small harbour at Polperro.

Fowey

ESTABLISHED
1904 (St Catherine's Point)

CURRENT TOWER
1904

OPERATOR
Fowey Harbour Commissioners

ACCESS
From the town centre, a short walk towards St Catherine's Head along the Esplanade Road will pass Whitehouse Point where the light is clearly visible; continue towards Readymoney Bay and take the South West Coast Path; after about a mile do not be confused by a small metal box surmounted by a red light beacon called St Catherine's Point Light on the walls of St Catherine's castle ruins, but continue to the lighthouse, which is on the seaward side of the path

The historic port of Fowey handles exports of china clay and is one of Cornwall's major ports. To mark a safe passage into the river Fowey, a series of navigation lights is operated by the harbour authority. The approach from the sea is marked by a lighthouse on the headland at St Catherine's Point, which is known as Fowey Entrance Light or Fowey Light, to avoid confusion with St Catherine's Point on the Isle of Wight.

In medieval times a light was displayed in the now demolished St Catherine's Chapel, but today the light is sited just to the west on the headland. Erected in 1904, this light is shown from a 20ft red cylindrical cast-iron lantern sitting on an octagonal concrete base with a white service building to the landward side. Through a letter box opening, it shows a white flashing light visible for eleven miles over the safe entry channel. To each side

▶ The cast-iron drum tower light at Whitehouse Point is situated on the west side of Fowey harbour.

▲ The light just to the west on the headland at the entrance to Fowey harbour.

it shows red flashing sector lights visible for nine miles.

The entry channel is marked by a light on the headland at Whitehouse Point which, when erected in 1904, was second-hand, having been manufactured in 1892. It consists of a red cast-iron cylinder with a letter box opening on top of a narrow red column. The area is surrounded by red iron railings, with a vertical external ladder up to the light. It shows a white flashing light visible for eight miles, with two sector lights, green to the right and red to the left. Electricity is supplied via an overhead cable from an adjacent dwelling. There is a simple red pole on the pier which carries two fixed red lights vertically above one another which are visible for eight miles.

Mevagissey

ESTABLISHED
1896

CURRENT TOWER
1896

OPERATOR
Mevagissey Harbour Trust

ACCESS
The outer harbour piers are open to the public

Despite Mevagissey's thriving fishing industry which had developed during the eighteenth century, the only protection was a medieval quay in the area now occupied by the East Quay. As this gave little protection from easterly gales, a group consisting of landowners and clergy, guided by several businessmen, proposed an approach be made to Parliament for a Harbour Act.

The first Harbour Act for Mevagissey was passed in 1774, when the East and West piers which form the inner harbour were built, but not until 1888 were the piers constructed to form what is now the outer harbour. Within three years the two outer piers were completely destroyed in bad , which resulted in the construction of the two Victorian outer piers that make up the current harbour.

The piers were not completed until 1897, but a lighthouse was constructed on the end of the south pier in 1896. Known as Mevagissey Victorian Pier Head Lighthouse, it consists of a white ornate 29ft hexagonal cast-iron tower with a gallery and lantern, and the lower part painted black. In keeping with the rest of the tower the lantern has an ornate top complete with weather vane.

The Harbour Trust was given charitable status in 1988 making it, along with Looe, one of only two registered harbour charities. It operates the lighthouse, whose light character is two white flashes every ten seconds, visible for twelve miles. The tower also carries a fog signal which sounds every thirty seconds in fog.

Although it is possible to drive to the pier, parking in the town and walking through the narrow streets to the outer harbour is a better option, particularly in the summer. A recommended alternative is to take the thirty-five minute trip boat journey between Fowey and Mevagissey to view the lights and daymark at Gribben Head from the sea.

▶▶ The ornate tower at the end of Mevagissey's south pier.

▼ An old postcard showing the lighthouse at the entrance to the small harbour.

St Anthony's

ESTABLISHED
1835

CURRENT TOWER
1835

AUTOMATED
1987

OPERATOR
Trinity House

ACCESS
Located at the end of Military Road off the A3078, reached via steep footpath from National Trust car park which is signposted from Trewithian; keepers' cottages can be rented as holiday homes

As early as the seventeenth century simple aids to navigation were employed to assist vessels entering Falmouth Harbour. The hazards in the area include the Manacles rocks off the southern approaches and the Black Rock in the centre of the channel. The town council petitioned Trinity House in 1830 for a light to be built, and the Corporation had a lighthouse designed by James Walker. Construction, which started in May 1834, was undertaken by Olver of Falmouth, with each stone shaped in Penzance and transported to the site by boat. Within a year, work was finished and the light was shown in 1835.

The location at St Anthony's Head was such a difficult one that it was treated as a rock station. The octagonal 62ft tower was built into the rock, with a raised area to the rear for the two-storey keepers' dwellings, and the lantern was blanked off at the rear by two chimney stacks. Thirty years after the light was commissioned, a large fog bell operated by automatic hammer was installed. This was replaced in 1882 by an even larger bell weighing two tons. Suspended from the gallery, it was replaced in 1954 by an electrical Nautophone foghorn on a platform. The bell was taken to Falmouth for display, but was subsequently melted down.

The light was originally provided through the catoptric system, with eight Argand lamps and parabolic reflectors which revolved by clockwork and were used to produce the flashing light. This was changed to petroleum vapour burner and eventually to electricity when mains power was installed in 1954. The fixed Fresnel lens showed an occulting white light, which was visible for twenty-two miles, with a red sector visible for twenty miles to mark the Manacles. It is battery powered, with the batteries charged from the mains electricity sypply.

The station was fully automated in 1987 and in 2000 was further modernised when the light configuration was changed to isophase.

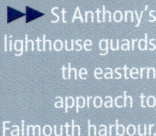
St Anthony's lighthouse guards the eastern approach to Falmouth harbour.

▶ The light was first shown from St Anthony's in April 1835.

Lizard

ESTABLISHED
1691

CURRENT TOWER
1752

AUTOMATED
1998

OPERATOR
Trinity House

ACCESS
The lighthouse is signposted from Lizard village

▶▶ The Lizard lighthouse, situated at the most southerly point in England, has guided vessels along the English Channel for almost four centuries and warns of the many hazards off Lizard Point.

▶ The Lizard lighthouse, dating from the early seventeenth century, is one of the oldest in the country. This old postcard shows the station when both towers were in operation.

The Lizard peninsula is the most southerly point in Britain, and its dangers to shipping are well known, with a series of jagged ridges of rock jutting out to sea for nearly 400 yards. The Lizard was used as a passage mark for ships wishing to dock in Falmouth or make passage up channel, and was therefore an ideal location for a lighthouse. Building a tower, however, was not easy, as locals were keen to hold on to revenues gained from salvaging cargoes from the many wrecks that occurred off the point.

As early as 1570 local landowner Sir John Killigrew was granted a patent to build a light, but local opposition stopped any action. In 1619 his grandson applied again for a patent and, despite the locals refusing assistance, built a coal-fired light. However, maintenance costs were prohibitive and with no income ensuing from dues, which passing ships only had to pay on a voluntary basis, the light was extinguished for periods in 1620 and 1621. Despite an appeal to the king, nothing was done to ease the cost burden and by 1630 the light was derelict.

In 1748 Richard Parish together with the then owner of Lizard Point, Thomas Fonnereau, applied to Trinity House for an agreement to build a total of four lights although, after protracted discussions, it was agreed only two were needed, so that the coast would be marked by a single light at St Agnes, a twin light at The Lizard and three lights at Casquets.

Even then the task of building the lights was not made easy by a strong difference of opinion between the two sides, which continued until 1771. Disagreements were over who should pay for what, whether the light should be extinguished should an enemy appear and, more importantly, who would own the lights. Nevertheless the twin lights, which can still be seen today, were completed and first lit on 22 August 1752.

Built on top of the original light, the twin 62ft eight-sided stone towers were joined by a block of two-storey dwellings. They were topped with a gallery

Lizard

▶▶ The operational tower at The Lizard is one of two which were built in 1752.

▼ The distinctive twin towers of the Lizard Lighthouse stand at either end of the service buildings and cottages. The active lighthouse is the south tower, while the north tower has had its lantern removed.

and wooden glazed lantern. Although the glazing reduced the light intensity, it considerably decreased the coal consumption. In 1771 Trinity House took over responsibility for the lighthouses. In 1812 the coal fires were replaced by Argand lamps and reflectors and the accommodation was modernised to give a corridor from one light to the other. In 1878 the Lizard became one of the earliest lighthouses to be converted to electricity with, it was claimed, the twin lights being some of the brightest in intensity anywhere.

In 1903 a revolving light was commissioned in the east tower and the light in the west tower was discontinued. The revolving light was so powerful that it could be seen beyond the horizon and, today, its reduced-power white flashing light with first order Fresnel lens is visible for twenty-six miles. The lantern on the west tower was removed and the tower itself remained unused. The station was automated and demanned in 1998, with the compressed air fog signal, the last in service, being replaced by an electric one.

Visitor facilities were operated by the Trevithick Trust until 2004, when the lighthouse was closed for renovations and the trust went out of operation. The lighthouse was awarded a grant by the Heritage Lottery Fund to develop its Heritage Centre, which opened in 2009 and provides new interpretation displays. The original engine room, the only such engine room still in existence, houses historic equipment as well as displays about the lighthouse itself and Trinity House's history.

Penzance

ESTABLISHED
1817 or 1818

CURRENT TOWER
1855

OPERATOR
Penzance Harbour Authority

ACCESS
Walking the pier, which is not restricted

▼ The light at Penzance harbour might be moved if plans to expand the harbour for a new ferry go ahead.

The current lighthouse at the end of the pier at Penzance dates from the harbour's rebuilding. Although the original pier, now called the South Pier, was constructed in 1785 with subsequent extensions in 1812 and in 1853, the lighthouse was not built until 1853. The Albert or North Pier was constructed in 1846 and was the second longest in Cornwall, exceeded only by that at Falmouth.

The first attempts to mark the harbour, which was once home to a large fishing fleet, came in either 1817 or 1818 when a light was exhibited on the end of the South Pier's first extension. However, it lasted only until February 1824, when a severe gale carried the top of the lighthouse away and severely damaged the pier. It was restored and remained in place until the new light was erected on the end of the new pier extension. There is little information about this light, but in 1853 John Mathews described it as being shown from a wooden shed at the pier end.

Shortly after the pier was extended in 1853 a new and much improved lighthouse was built on its terminal. Commissioned on 1 August 1855, the 31ft iron tower was cast by Sandy & Co at the Copperhouse Foundry in Hayle. The lantern, made of sheet steel, is mounted on a square cast-iron pedestal and has a white conical roof which supports a weather vane. It was fitted with a fifth order lens, which was a great improvement on the Argand lamp in the old light. The white flashing light had a sector light which steered vessels clear of the Gear Rock and the Raymond.

Sperm oil was used in bad weather as it burned for longer, so the keeper did not have to stay overnight. The lighthouse was modernised in 1914, when a new, more powerful 1,000 candle-power electric light was installed. The flashing light, which is red to each side to mark the Gear Rock with a white inner sector to mark the safe channel, is visible for nine miles.

Newlyn

ESTABLISHED	1887
CURRENT TOWER	1905
OPERATOR	Newlyn Pier and Harbour Commission
ACCESS	The south pier is closed so the light has to be viewed from the 1,760ft Victoria Pier

Lying to the western side of Mount's Bay, Newlyn is a busy fishing port. The first of the piers that form today's harbour, the 600ft south pier, was built in 1884. In 1887 a lighthouse was completed at its end, and was first exhibited in March 1887. In 1914 the pier was extended by 100ft and a new lighthouse on the end was first lit on 29 April 1915. This white 34ft circular cast-iron tower has a round lantern complete with gallery. The cupola and the base of the tower are painted red. The light, flashing every five seconds, has a range of nine miles.

A Nautophone fog siren sounds a four-second blast every sixty seconds, and is used when the fishing fleet is at sea.

The red and white building alongside, also built in 1914, houses the Ordnance Survey datum equipment as this location is the starting point for all their geographic data. On the end of the north or Victoria Pier a simple light on top of a cast-iron column shows a fixed white light, which is visible for four miles, with a green sector marking the safe channel. There are also simple fixed red lights on the end of the Old Quay and Inner Quay.

◀ The light at the end of Newlyn's south pier dates from the late nineteenth century.

Tater Du

ESTABLISHED	1965
CURRENT TOWER	1965
AUTOMATED	1965, fully automated 1996-7
OPERATOR	Trinity House
ACCESS	Via South West Coast Path; tower closed

▶▶ Tater Du lighthouse takes its name from an old Cornish term for black rock. The main light is visible for twenty-three miles.

▼ Tater Du was the first automatic lighthouse to be built with a high intensity light and the first in England for sixty years.

Although the Runnelstone Rocks, which lie just offshore, have been marked by a buoy, and Gwennap Head by beacons since the eighteenth century, it was not until the Spanish ship Juan Ferrar was wrecked off Boscawen Point in 1963 with the loss of eleven lives that a lighthouse in the Boscawen area was seen as a pressing requirement.

The Newlyn and Mousehole Fishermen's' Association wrote to Trinity House suggesting a light on Tater-Du or Carn Boscawen. The Corporation considered whether to provide a small local light to guide vessels into harbour or a more powerful one for general navigational needs. They chose the latter and the location Tater Du.

Built by Humphries between 1964 and 1965 to the design of Michael H. Crisp, this automatic lighthouse was constructed from white concrete blocks and consists of a 50ft circular tower with a gallery and small lantern mounted on the roof of a rectangular service building.

As the site was inaccessible, a long steep access road was constructed from the top of the Rosemodress cliffs. The tower was officially opened on 7 July 1965 by HRH Duke of Gloucester, who ceremoniously pressed a button to start the light. The main light is a Fourth Order 250mm rotating optic which, powered by a seventy-watt lamp, shows a white light giving three flashes every fifteen seconds.

About 10ft lower is a sector light covering the Runnelstone Rocks, which shows a fixed red light visible for thirteen miles. Power to the lights is via batteries continually recharged from the mains. In the event of a power failure the batteries will operate for five days, but there is also a stand-by generator.

Longships

ESTABLISHED
1795

CURRENT TOWER
1873

AUTOMATED
1988

OPERATOR
Trinity House

ACCESS
Can only be viewed by boat

Looking from Land's End towards the Isles of Scilly on a tranquil summer's day can hide the dangerous nature of the area in stormy weather. The rocky outcrops about a mile out to sea present a formidable obstacle, especially when the Atlantic throws its might landwards, completely submerging the reefs, on which many ships and vessels have been lost.

By 1787 Trinity House were being pressed by various bodies to provide a suitable light in the vicinity of Land's End to mark the rocks. In 1790 John Smeaton was commissioned to survey the area and he suggested a lighthouse on either Wolf Rock or Longships, or even a site on Roseveern near the Scillies. He also pointed out the great cost and the possible consequence of failure.

In 1794 Trinity House, at the time supporting private lighthouses, gave Lieut Henry Smith a patent to build a tower on either Wolf Rock or Longships. After consideration, Smith chose Longships, considering the Wolf Rock alternative to be too expensive. He erected a number of beacons on Longships, but these were soon washed away. He initially surrendered the lease, but having second thoughts he commissioned architect Samuel Wyatt to design a tower for him.

The site chosen by Wyatt was Carn Bass rock, the highest point on the Longships Reef. As Wyatt had already undertaken work for Trinity House, getting his design approved was straightforward, and so his tower was built Completed in 1795, it was lit for the first time on 29 September.

It was a 28ft tapered circular tower of three storeys beneath a wooden and copper lantern, which held eighteen parabolic reflectors and Argand lamps in two tiers. In order to save oil, no lights were shown to landward, with that side of the lantern blanked off. Later that year, Smith was declared incapable of managing the light, and sent to jail as a bankrupt. Although

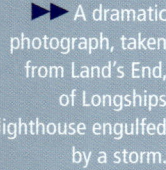

▶▶ A dramatic photograph, taken from Land's End, of Longships lighthouse engulfed by a storm.

▶ A nineteenth century engraving showing the first Longships lighthouse.

Longships

▲ The 1873-built Longships tower before automation.

▶▶ The Longships lighthouse after the solar panels and a new emergency generator had been fitted.

Trinity House then took over, the Corporation continued to pay him and later his family the substantial light dues until 1836 when, empowered by Act of Parliament, the Corporation bought out the remaining nine years of the lease for £40,676.

Even though it was in place for almost seventy years, the light was not a total success, with the sea often breaking over it or the light being obscured by spray, so various shipowners petitioned for an improved light. After years of prevarication, Trinity House had a new tower built alongside the existing one in 1873 under the guidance of Sir James Douglass. At 115ft, the circular grey granite tower was considerably taller and thus eliminated the earlier problems. A helical lantern by Chance Brothers was fitted and originally it had a concial roof, but in 1974 this was replaced by a helipad. The old lighthouse, retained during construction of the new one, was never actually demolished because, shortly after the new light had been commissioned, it slid into the sea.

The new light, first lit on 3 December 1873, was a first order dioptric apparatus with a Douglass multiwick fountain oil lamp with a character of five seconds lit with a five-second eclipse. The white light, visible for twenty miles, had a red sector over Runnelstone Rock. In 1904 the lamp was replaced with an incandescent oil burner.

In 1925 the light intensity was increased by the installation of a Hood autoform incandescent oil burner. In 1967 the lighthouse was converted to diesel-powered electrical operation. Today, the white isophase light is visible for eighteen miles to sea, with a red sector visible for fourteen miles marking the safe fair weather passage to the landward side of the rocks. The lighthouse was automated in 1988 and in 2005 converted to solar power.

Because the light was often obscured by sea spray it was equipped with a fog bell. This was replaced by a rocket fog signal apparatus in the 1890s. In 1904, when the light was being upgraded, this was replaced by a Matthews fog apparatus, which gives one blast every ten seconds.

Wolf Rock

ESTABLISHED
1795

CURRENT TOWER
1870

AUTOMATED
1988

OPERATOR
Trinity House

ACCESS
Can only be viewed by boat

Ten miles south-west of Land's End stands a pinnacle of rock which takes its name from the fact that a chimney of rock filled and emptied of water as the waves ebbed and flowed made a howling sound like a wolf. It is reputed that local wreckers filled it with stones to stop seafarers being warned of the rock's presence. These same people also opposed the placing of a bell buoy near the rock in 1750 as it would make a noise and frighten away the fish.

In 1791 a proposal to build a stone lighthouse on the rock came to nothing as Lieut Henry Smith, the builder of Longstone lighthouse, thought it beyond his ability. He did erect a 20ft wrought iron mast supporting a model of a wolf in 1795, but this was washed away. In a four-year construction period from 1836 to 1840 a hollow iron-coned beacon filled with rubble was erected on the rock by James Walker, which remains to this day. But this was just a temporary solution as it was only visible during daylight and even then was hard to see.

So in 1861, following the successful design of Smeaton's Eddystone tower, James Walker commenced work on a 115ft granite stone tower. To avoid deterioration of the joint material due to wave action, for the lower 35ft the upper surface of each stone was given a wide rabbit and the stone above dropped into the recess, thus protecting the joints from the sea. The stones were dressed at the depot in Penzance and taken out to the rock at such a painstakingly slow pace that it was eight years before the tower was completed and a further year before, in 1870, a light was displayed.

During the initial construction process, when each gang arrived for a day's work, one of the men had to swim to the rock with a rope and it was not until 1864, after the masons had fixed enough foundation stones to the rock, using iron bolts, that a landing area could be constructed. This landing stage was equipped with a crane, which enabled the stone blocks to be hauled onto the rock, thus greatly speeding up the construction work. In addition, a steam-powered winch was erected on the partially completed tower and the time taken to hoist each stone into place was reduced from about fifteen minutes to less than three.

An indication of the size of the operation can be appreciated by the fact that the diameter of the tower is 42ft at the base tapering to 18ft at the top. The tower required at total of 3,300 tons of granite and the landing stage 1,100 tons. The flashing red and white lights, visible for sixteen miles, were converted from paraffin to electrical operation in 1955, when diesel engines were installed.

The lighthouse is noted for being the first in Britain to be equipped with a helipad, the design of which became the prototype for others. In 1988 the station was demanned and now the only access is via helicopter.

▶ The impressive Wolf Rock tower entered service in January 1870 and lies almost five miles south-west of Land's End.

Wolf Rock

▲ The daymarks on Gwennap Head erected in 1821.

▶▶ The impressive Wolf Rock light on a calm day.

▼ Wolf Rock tower was the first to be fitted with a helipad.

While it was manned, there were two notable incidents. The first occurred in January 1948 when storms on the south coast made it impossible to relieve any of the rock lighthouses. When the keepers on Wolf Rock were twenty-two days overdue to be relieved, they managed to signal to the passing vessel Scillonian that they were low on supplies. Trinity House's attempts to send them by sea failed as the waves were half way up the tower. But on 5 February, using considerable skill, a helicopter pilot managed to land supplies and ten days later the station was relieved.

The second incident came on 18 December 1969 and had a tragic ending as a keeper disappeared when fishing from the winch room. Although the barriers were all still in place, he disappeared and his body has never been found.

At the time the beacons were first erected on Wolf Rock, similar structures were erected on the Runnelstone rock a mile offshore. These beacons were subsequently washed away and it was only the fact that the rock surface was of insufficient size to support a tower that a lighthouse was also not erected there.

In the event, in 1821 two daymarks were erected on Gwennap Head which, when in line, mark the position of the rock. Both are 12ft with the southern mark consisting of a red cone with the north, or landward, one a black and circular tower with a conical roof mounted on a square base. Today the rock is marked by a black and yellow buoy showing a white flashing light. The daymarks are both accessible from the South West Coast Path by walking west from the Porthgwarra car park.

Peninnis, Scilly

ESTABLISHED
1911

CURRENT TOWER
1911

OPERATOR
Trinity House

ACCESS
Walking from Hugh Town, St Mary's

▶ The lighthouse at Peninnis is the only such tower on St Mary's, the largest of the Isles of Scilly.

▼ The 45ft steel tower at Peninnis has a small white and green service building to one side.

Although it is the principle Island of the Isles of Scilly, St Mary's was not one of the first islands to have a lighthouse. In 1716 William Whiston proposed a revolutionary Ball of Fire or Light be thrown into the air four times during darkness with one timed at midnight. He suggested a light range of sixty miles and a sound range of twenty miles. His navigational aid would be distinguishable from St Agnes and other lights in the area, but his idea came to nothing, and not until 1911 did the island eventually get a lighthouse.

The light, located on the outer headland at Peninnis Head, is at the most southerly point of the island. It helps vessels entering St Mary's Sound and into Hugh Town harbour. Built to replace St Agnes light, it consists of a white circular 45ft steel tower on an open lattice foundation. The lantern has a white gallery with a black-domed top. Unmanned since its inception, the white light flashes every fifteen seconds and is visible for sixteen miles.

Peninnis was one of the first gas-powered stations: the original light source was acetylene with a unique gas-powered optic. In 1992 it was converted to electricity. The light can be seen by walking about a mile and a half along the headland from Hugh Town. The only other light on the island is a simple harbour light visible for three miles on a pole at Hugh Town pier. It was originally white, but in 1907 was replaced by a red light that stood 6ft higher.

At night a vantage point on the east of the island shows up the V-shaped light configuration of the lights round the mainland.

Round Island, Scilly

ESTABLISHED
1887

CURRENT TOWER
1887

OPERATOR
Trinity House

ACCESS
Trip boats from Hugh Town, on St Mary's, pass the island, but landing on it is restricted

▶▶ Round Island lighthouse is located on the most northerly of the Scilly Isles, north-east of Tresco

▶ The lighthouse complex on Round Island showing the keepers' quarters near the tower. Despite its elevation, severe gales in January 1984 whipped up seas which smashed the lower doors of the fog-signal house.

Round Island, to the north-east of Tresco, is the most northerly point on the Isles of Scilly where a lighthouse could be located and the barren, wave-battered rock has only ever been inhabited by lighthouse keepers. The Island has enough room to accommodate not only a conventional lighthouse with separate keepers' quarters, but also a small garden and a separate helipad.

The lighthouses is one of those dating from the latter half of the nineteenth century when Trinity House was expanding its operations and building many new stations. Constructing the station on Round Island, however, proved particularly challenging as the rock is over 130ft above sea level and surrounded by precipitous sides. So, despite the island being relatively large, Trinity House found the process of transporting the building materials to the site, up the cliff face and onto the rock, as difficult as at a true rock station.

The 63ft white circular tower, complete with a lantern and balcony, was designed by Sir James Douglass. The tower was completed in 1887 and, unusually, exhibited a red flashing light. Because red has weaker propagation qualities than white, the light was intensified by a huge hyperradial lens of a sort only fitted to two other Trinity House lights. This optic was replaced in 1967 by more modern apparatus, which was in turn replaced in 1987 when the light was automated and changed to flashing white. The white single-storey keepers' dwelling, now a service block, is separat, but linked by a corridor to the light tower with a fog signal room nearby.

On the adjacent island of St Martin's, at St Martin's Head, is a 40ft red and white conical stone tower built by Thomas Elkins in 1683. This two-storey tower is now a daymark. Although the doorway is blocked, the tower is hollow with a stone stairway to the upper floor which has two windows. It was used as a watchtower, or may even have shown a light at some point.

St Agnes, Scilly

ESTABLISHED
1680

CURRENT TOWER
1680

DISCONTINUED
1911

ACCESS
Trip boats from St Mary's go to St Agnes, and the lighthouse, which is visible from most parts of the island, can easily be reached on foot

The lighthouse on St Agnes was constructed by Trinity House in 1680, making it one of the Corporation's earliest lighthouses. The four-storey 74ft white tower, with a lantern and gallery complete with attached dwellings, was erected on the highest point of the small island by Captains Hugh Hill and Simon Bayly after the idea for a light on St Agnes had been first suggested to Trinity House by Sir John Clayton in the 1660s.

The tower was of substantial construction, with walls 6ft thick at their base and best English heart oak used throughout. It was the most important lighthouse undertaken by Trinity House at the time, but the high cost of building materials proved so expensive that Trinity House became impoverished.

The lantern, reached by a wooden stair starting at the first floor, was carried on a shallow stone vault, although the original lantern floor was of timber construction, as are the lower floors. A stone mural stair gave access to the first floor, which was lit by four gun-ports. The Scillies, by their location, were at the mercy of marauders, including pirates, and so building in some defensive measures to the light tower was natural.

The light was initially provided from a coal fire enclosed in a lantern, with a funnel in the roof, and this is the earliest instance of an enclosed coal fire. However, despite the ventilation, the enclosed light caused problems with the glass quickly being covered by soot. Another problem was caused by the local keepers who were neither always sober enough nor inclined to properly maintain the light.

The situation improved in 1790, when the lighthouse was converted to oil, with a parabolic reflector making the flashing white light visible for eighteen miles. But its usefulness was relatively short-lived. In 1858 the Bishop Rock light was completed to cover the area to the west and from 1911 Peninnis on St Mary's performed a similar function for the eastern area. The St Agnes light was therefore discontinued.

▶▶ The historic tower at St Agnes has two attached dwellings which are now leased, with the tower itself retained as a daymark. The original grate from the lighthouse is on display as a feature in Tresco gardens.

▶ An old postcard showing visitors to St Agnes in the early years of the twentieth century.

Bishop Rock, Scilly

ESTABLISHED
1858

CURRENT TOWER
1887

AUTOMATED
1991

OPERATOR
Trinity House

ACCESS
Trip boats operate out of Hugh Town on St Mary's to the rock

▶▶ The impressive Bishop Rock lighthouse.

▶ Bishop Rock lighthouse before the helipad was added.

The presence of a lighthouse on St Agnes provided a degree of security to vessels approaching the Isles of Scilly, but the light's position did not give adequate warning from the west and many vessels foundered on the rocks before the St Agnes light was visible. In 1847 Trinity House decided to rectify this, and Engineer-in-Chief James Walker began to erect a light on the Bishop Rock, largest of the westerly outcrops, he proposed a similar structure to that on the Smalls in iron. This iron-legged structure, designed to offer minimal resistance to heavy seas, was within days of having its lantern installed when, during a severe storm in February 1850, it was washed away.

Undaunted, Walker then designed a circular granite tower 150ft tall, complete with lantern and gallery, similar to the Eddystone light. Taking seven years to complete, this structure was supervised on site by James Douglass. The 2,500 tons of interlocking granite blocks were dressed and assembled on the mainland before being shipped out to the rock. The light, visible for sixteen miles, was first shown on 1 September 1858 and was successful in reducing but not eliminating shipwrecks.

However, the tower was not a total success as at times it was obscured by spray and suffered damage in the frequent storms. The keepers also became increasingly concerned about the state of the foundations, which had been anchored to a relatively small cross section of rock. It was therefore decided that a completely new tower should be built outside the existing one, with a large round granite stone base attached to the rock by iron bolts as a firm foundation.

The new tower was built between 1883 and 1887 and increased the tower's height to 162ft. The flashing white light, visible for twenty-four miles, was first shown in October 1887. The optic was fuelled by a paraffin burner until electrified in 1973. In 1976 a helipad was added and relieving the keepers by helicopter was much easier, as relief by sea was impossible in anything but calm weather.

Pendeen

ESTABLISHED
1900

CURRENT TOWER
1900

OPERATOR
Trinity House

ACCESS
The lighthouse is situated at Pendeen near St Just with parking adjacent to the outer wall

▶▶ The Pendeen lighthouse guards Cornwall's north coast between Land's End and Godrevy Island.

▼ An old postcard showing Pendeen lighthouse and fog signal in the early twentieth century.

The stretch of coast from Cape Cornwall to St Ives Bay is particularly inhospitable. The Three Stone Oar off Pendeen and Gurnard's Head at the western entrance of St Ives Bay are the principal dangers to shipping, but it was not until the late nineteenth century that a lighthouse was built to warn of these hazards. Until then, maritime safety depended on a rocket apparatus at the Coastguard Station and the lifeboats stationed at Sennen Cove, Hayle and St Ives.

The high cliffs along this coastline prevented passing vessels from catching sight of either Trevose Head or Longships and so many were lost, unable to determine their position. Sunken and exposed rocks near Pendeen Watch proved particularly hazardous, and this was brought to the attention of Trinity House as the nineteenth century drew to a close. The Corporation decided to erect a lighthouse and fog signal at Pendeen at a time when it was increasing the number of aids to navigation under the principle of having a major light every twenty miles.

Pendeen light was designed by Sir Thomas Matthews, Trinity House Engineer, and construction was undertaken by Arthur Carkeek of Redruth, with the lantern supplied by Chance Bros of Birmingham. Before work on the buildings could begin, the cap of the Point had to be removed and the headland flattened. A retaining wall was completed on the seaward side and then the buildings, which occupy a large area, were completed. Although Carkeek's men had only reached the halfway mark by the start of 1900, the lantern was ready and work progressed more rapidly until the light was commissioned on 26 September 1900.

The 56ft squat circular tower is white-painted, built of rubble stone cement and divided into two rooms, one over the other. Above them is the lantern, which originally contained a five-wick Argand lamp to which oil was pumped from the room below. An electric lamp was installed in 1926 and the original oil lamp was later displayed at the now-closed Trinity House National Lighthouse Centre in Penzance. Around the lamp revolves an apparatus, containing the lenses, which floats in a trough of mercury so that it can be moved by the slightest touch.

Pendeen was automated in 1995 and the keepers left on 3 May. The original optic has been retained, with a range of sixteen nautical miles, but a new lamp plinth has been installed along with an emergency light and a new fog signal with fog detector.

St Ives

ESTABLISHED
circa 1538

CURRENT TOWER
1890

OPERATOR
Penwith District Council

ACCESS
The East Pier has public access and the lighthouses can be easily approached

▶▶ The lighthouse at the end of Smeaton's Pier shows two fixed vertical green lights.

▼ The lighthouse on St Ives' East Pier, built in 1830, was deactivated in 1890 and restored in the late 1990s after almost being destroyed by fire in 1996.

Although St Ives had the largest fishing fleet in Penrith district in the fourteenth century, it did not have a harbour until 1770. It can however claim to have one of the earliest lights in Cornwall. In 1538 John Leland was quoted as saying there was a pharos 'on the Chapel of St Nicholas on the point of Pendinas', the island to the northern side of the town. In addition, it is probable that a beacon, which could be lit when an enemy approached, was erected nearby. Later, a light consisting of a lantern on a pole was displayed on what is now called Lamp Rock.

The first section of the East Pier was built between 1766 and 1770 under John Smeaton's supervision, but not until 1830 did James and Edward Harvey build a lighthouse on the pier's end. It consisted of a square stone base with an octagonal stone gallery room, as distinct from a lantern room.

The top section offered an observation area and was topped by a black-domed roof with a weather vane. The light in this 20ft building was converted to gas in 1835 and was then visible for seven miles. It was, however, only used until 1890, becoming redundant when the pier was lengthened; it is now located halfway along the extended pier.

When the pier was extended, a new light was erected on the end. This 32ft octagonal cast-iron tower was prefabricated by Stothert and Pitt in Bath and was brought to the site to be mounted on a black base. The remainder of the tower, including the domed top, is white. The light showed fixed red, with a white sector to the south when there was above 10ft of water, which changed to green when there was less than 10ft.

Hayle

ESTABLISHED
1840

CURRENT TOWER
1840

ACCESS
Can be reached by following the South West Coast Path on foot, alongside the railway line, with parking available near the cemetery

The small town of Hayle developed during the industrial expansion of the eighteenth and nineteenth centuries serving Cornwall's mining industry. Two companies, Cornish Copper Company and Harvey & Co, expanded Hayle harbour, but the rivalry between the two was so great that it split the town in two, with workers from one company having nothing to do with the other. The former, founded in 1756, built quays and a canal in the Copperhouse Pool area, while the latter had their smelting works near Penpol Creek and built the South Quay in 1819.

However, as the mining declined so did the rivalry, and heavy engineering became a main source of employment. Even this trade had disappeared by the end of the First World War, and with a continual reduction in trade the port was closed in 1985. But the harbour remains well used and a steady stream of pleasure craft continue to enter the river, guided into the estuary by a series of perch poles mounted along the training wall.

In addition, two lights are sited on the western side of the river entrance which, when in line, mark a safe channel. The rear light, a replacement for the original light of 1840, consists of a square concrete box with a flat roof mounted on four legs, with four concrete stays, one on each side. The white-painted structure has a red horizontal band across the middle and shows a fixed white light visible for four miles through a window in the seaward side. Situated 120 yards in front is a similar structure with similar light characteristics. They are located in the sand dunes on the golf course at Lelant.

▶ The rear light at Hayle is red and white to act as a daymark for vessels using the river.

▶ The small rear light at Hayle is at the edge of the golf course above the sand dunes.

Portreath

ESTABLISHED	1812
DISCONTINUED	Unknown
ACCESS	The harbour and pier are open to the public

The lighthouse at Portreath dates from the early nineteenth century when the area was a centre for copper mining. The harbour was extended by Francis Basset of Tehidy so that it could be used for both copper exports as well as importing coal, which was needed to power the steam engines in the mines.

A squat circular stone tower, which had a light on its flat roof, was constructed in 1812 at the end of Landmark Pier, a new jetty constructed on the harbour's west side. To mark the entrance, a 25ft white conical daymark was erected on the hill above the west side of the harbour, which is still in use but no longer displays tide signals and the weather vane has been removed. As Gull Rock and Horse Rock presented such a hazard to sailing ships, a castellated lookout was erected near the daymark with another lookout on the end of the east wall in the harbour.

◀ The daymark on the top of the hill is the most distinctive of the aids to navigation around Portreath's small harbour. The squat white-painted lighthouse of 1812 at the end of the jetty has long since been defunct.

Godrevy Island

ESTABLISHED
1859

CURRENT TOWER
1859

AUTOMATED
1939

OPERATOR
Trinity House

ACCESS
Reached only by boat, but can easily be seen from the coast path

Godrevy Island, three and a half miles across St Ives Bay and partly covered with grass as it slopes down to the sea, is home to a number of seabirds and flora despite often taking the full force of Atlantic gales. The island's lighthouse was built to mark a dangerous reef, called the Stones, which extends outwards towards St Ives, on which many vessels have been wrecked.

The disaster which resulted in the lighthouse being built occurred on 30 November 1854, when the iron screw steamer Nile was totally wrecked on the reef with the loss of all passengers and crew. Within two months a number of petitions had been raised and these were presented to Trinity House with the aim of getting a lighthouse erected.

Tenders for the construction work were received and by December 1857 the contract had been finalised. James Sutcliffe was appointed as the residential engineer for the project, and supervised the construction work. The station was designed by James Walker and was completed at a cost of £7,082 15s 7d.

Its light was first exhibited on 1 March 1859.

The white octagonal 120ft tower was made from rubble stone bedded in mortar, and was sited, together with its adjoining keepers' cottages, almost in the centre of the largest of the rocks that make up the island. The original optic revolved on rollers and was driven by a clockwork motor. This motor was in turn driven by a large weight running down a cavity in the tower's wall.

Two keepers were originally appointed to maintain the two lights, one flashing white every ten seconds, and the other a fixed red light, which marked the Stones Rocks. The lights had a range of seventeen and fifteen miles respectively. The keepers' tours of duty were two months on and one month off.

The station was equipped with a bell as a fog signal, which sounded once every five seconds. The station was automated and altered in 1939, when a new second-order fixed catadioptric lens was installed. The fog bell was removed and the keepers withdrawn at the same time.

▶▶ The lighthouse at Godrevy Island, at the north-eastern entrance to St Ives Bay, was completed in 1859.

▶ Godrevy lighthouse before the keepers' cottages were demolished.

Trevose Head

ESTABLISHED
1847

CURRENT TOWER
1847

AUTOMATED
1995

OPERATOR
Trinity House

ACCESS
There is a signed toll road from the B3276 with parking nearby; the coast path also passes the station

▶▶ The impressive lighthouse at Trevose Head dates from the middle of the nineteenth century.

▼ Trevose Head lighthouse and keepers' accommodation from the air.

Somewhat surprisingly, in the early 1800s only two lights, those at Longships and Lundy Island, marked the dangerous North Cornwall coast, guiding ships using the Bristol Channel. Although the Padstow area had been considered by Trinity House for a light in 1813 and 1832, not until 1847 was one built. Trevose Head, to the west of the river Camel, was chosen for a new station and two lights were erected on the headland.

Built by Jacob and Thomas Olver, of Falmouth, the high light consisted of an 89ft circular tower on a stone base with gallery and lantern. The fixed white light, visible for twenty miles, shone towards the north-east and was powered by a wick oil lamp made by H. Wilkins & Sons of London. The large first order dioptric system was manufactured by Henry Lepaute. Two pairs of single-storey dwellings, joined to the tower by a corridor, were constructed.

To identify the light as Trevose, a second light was built and was first exhibited just before the high light first shone. Situated about 50ft in front of the high light, it was connected to it by a corridor and, because of the slope to the ground, the lantern was at the same height as the base of the high light. It too exhibited a fixed white light through a similar apparatus, and was visible for seventeen miles.

As the lights were still difficult to distinguish, the characteristic of the high light was changed in 1882 to occulting and the low light was discontinued; it was subsequently demolished. A further change took place at the turn of the century, when the light was altered to flash red by the installation of red panels.

Between 1911 and 1913 the station, including the keepers' dwellings, was modernised. A new first order catadioptric lens with three symmetrical panels was installed and, in about

Trevose Head

▲ Trevose Head lighthouse overlooks the North Atlantic.

▶▶ Close-up view of the tower at Trevose Head, which is situated about five miles north-west of Padstow. When the keepers' houses were vacated in 1995, they were converted into holiday homes.

▶ Trevose Head lighthouse showing the 36ft long foghorn trumpet which was installed in 1913.

1920, a new type of Hood oil vapour burner complete with an autoform mantle was installed in this lens. This gave satisfactory service until 1974, when the station was electrified.

The lens mechanism, which was driven by weights installed in 1912, was retained until the station was demanned in 1995. The original optic was also retained, but the red panels were removed to give a white flashing light, which was powered by a metal halide lamp mounted in a two-position lamp changer. As an emergency stand-by light, a Tideland ML300 lantern with a range of ten miles was mounted on the gallery railings.

The area is prone to fog and so, during a refit in 1913, a new type of foghorn was installed in a specially-built fog signal house. It consisted of a trumpet 36ft long with an aperture measuring 18ft by 2ft devised to give a wide horizontal spread. In 1963 this was replaced by a supertyphon air-driven fog signal with eight horns. When the station was demanned in 1995 the fog signal was changed from an air-operated system to an electrically-operated omnidirectional one, giving two blasts every thirty seconds.

The entry into Padstow harbour over the Doom Bar is treacherous and, coupled with the many rocks in the vicinity of Stepper Point to the west and Pentire Point to the east, ships often foundered in trying to make Padstow. So in 1829, an Association for the Preservation of Life and Property from Shipwreck was formed.

One of the Association's actions was to erect a square tapered daymark, 40ft high, on the headland to the west of Stepper Point which, on a clear day, can be seen for more than twenty miles. A barrel on a pole at Stepper Point was also erected, but this no longer exists. In its place is an automatic fixed white light. A similar light is located on the other shore at St Saviour's Point, while Padstow Harbour has two vertical lights on poles.

Hartland Point

ESTABLISHED
1874

CURRENT TOWER
1874

AUTOMATED
1984

OPERATOR
Trinity House

ACCESS
Can be viewed from the coast path

▶▶ Hartland Point lighthouse was built in 1874 on a large rock outcrop.

▼ Hartland lighthouse looking over the helipad constructed in 1984.

Hartland Point lighthouse, about three miles north-west of Hartland, guides vessels approaching the Bristol Channel and marks the passage between the Devon coast and Lundy Island. The lighthouse, situated at the tip of the point below the cloud base, was built by Yerward of Wales under the supervision of Trinity House engineer Sir James Douglass and the surveyor, Mr Beasley.

The light housed in the 57ft brick tower consisted of a Chance Bros revolving dioptric lantern showing red and white flashes every thirty seconds with a range of seventeen miles. The station was blessed by the Bishop of Exeter, Frederick Temple, and the light was lit for the first time by Lady Stuckley of Hartland Abbey during the opening ceremony on 1 July 1874.

During the early twentieth century the station was threatened by the undermining action of the sea. Trinity House therefore had to have the rock broken away from the cliff head behind the lighthouse so that it fell on the beach and formed a barrier against the waves. The original deposits were washed away whenever a north-westerly gale coincided with a high spring tide. So in 1925 a permanent barrier and sea wall 100ft long and 20ft high, was constructed to solve the problem.

The station was automated in 1984, having been manned by four keepers who lived with their families in dwellings attached to the lighthouse. The dwellings were then demolished, making space for a helipad next to the tower which greatly improved access to the station as the access road was liable to frequent rock falls and landslips.

The 2010 Aids to Navigation Review undertaken by Trinity House proposed to discontinue the Hartland Point lighthouse on the grounds that global positioning systems had made this, and a number of other lighthouses, redundant. However, the closure of what was seen as one of North Devon's most famous landmarks was met with much local opposition and led to Trinity House agreeing to continue the light at reduced power. In 2011 they installed a solar power system powering a reduced power navigational beacon.

River Tawe

CROW POINT
ESTABLISHED 1820
CURRENT TOWER 1954
AUTOMATED 1984
OPERATOR Trinity House
ACCESS Via the nature reserve toll and car park on Braunton Sands

The rivers Taw and Torridge meet and flow into Bideford or Barnstaple Bay between the sand dunes of Northam to the south and Braunton to the north. To guide ships through this area, the channel for which can only be negotiated at half tide, four lighthouses were constructed by Trinity House in 1820.

Braunton High • To guide ships over the treacherous bar, a pair of lights was erected on the Braunton side of the estuary near Crow Point. These lights were called Braunton High and Low but were often referred to as Braunton Sands or Bideford Lights and latterly as Crow Point light. The original high light was situated on the river bank about 100 yards from Crow Point; it was a unique 86ft octagonal wooden tower protruding through the roof of a wooden keeper's dwelling supported by a wooden strut from the tower to each corner of the dwellings roof. White with a red stripe on the seaward side it originally showed the light through a window in the tower but later it was complete with a gallery and conical-roofed lantern. The fixed white light was visible for fifteen miles. It was built by Joseph Nelson in 1820 and altered in 1889, but it became unstable in 1945 and was demanned, being superseded in 1954.

Braunton Low • The low light was also built in 1820 and again, for Trinity House, was unusual. It consisted of a 15ft high close boarded hut on wooden legs with the light displayed through a window. Situated about 300 yards to the north it, like the high light, was painted white with a red stripe and displayed a fixed white light visible for fourteen miles. It was altered in 1832 and 1902. Because the channel could only be navigated above half tide, there was a ball on a mast which the keeper raised when the tide was sufficient to enter. This was later altered to a red

▶▶ The modern Crow Point light, which flashes every five seconds, white or red depending on direction, is located opposite Instow at Braunton Sands. The range lights at Instow can be seen in the background.

▶ The old Braunton High light, sometimes called Bideford, was superseded in 1954 and demolished in 1957. The lights were called Braunton High and Low, but were often referred to as Braunton Sands or Bideford.

River Tawe

INSTOW

ESTABLISHED
1820

CURRENT TOWER
????????

OPERATOR
Torridge District Council

ACCESS
The high light is visible from the bypass and the low light from the car park in Anstey Way

and green light system. This light was deactivated in 1954 and demolished in 1957.

Crow Point • In 1954 a new automatic light called Crow Point was erected to replace the 1820 lights. It was mounted on a 25ft square skeleton tower with a gallery but no lantern. The flashing red or white light every five seconds, dependant on direction, was originally acetylene powered, but in 1987 it was converted to solar power with a 300mm fixed drum optic and was modernised in 2001.

Instow Front • Because the channel from the sea to the junction of the two rivers is so difficult Trinity House erected a pair of range lights at Instow on the east side of the estuary in 1820 to mark the narrow passage. The Front Range light consisted of a wooden tower near to the river bank. It was replaced in 1964 by the current 58ft tall open lattice tower on the roof of a small equipment hut. There is a white daymark near the top of the tower with a sealed beam light unit giving an occulting white light every six seconds visible for fifteen miles mounted in a gallery on top.

Instow Rear • Situated on the hillside to the east of the village bypass road, the Rear Range light was mounted on a tubular steel structure. It was replaced in 1964 by the current 28ft skeleton tower mounted on the roof of a square concrete hut. The tower has a large white daymark on the seaward side and supports a sealed beam light on an open lattice gallery. The occulting white light every ten seconds is visible for fifteen miles. Both the original light structures were surrendered to Christie Estate Trust on 8 August 1966 for use at Braunton Burrows Nature Reserve.

▼ The range lights at Instow, erected in 1964, as seen from Crow Point Light.

▲ The Front Range light at Instow was erected in 1964 to replace the 1820 light, which was situated slightly closer to the river.

◀ The Rear Range light at Instow, erected in 1964, is situated on the hillside to the east of the bypass road.

Bull Point

ESTABLISHED
1879

CURRENT TOWER
1976

AUTOMATED
1976

OPERATOR
Trinity House

ACCESS
Via the coast path from Mortehoe

▶▶ The modern lighthouse at Bull Point dates from the 1970s.

▼ The Bull Point lighthouse of 1879, which was destroyed by clifftop erosion in the September 1972.

The headland to the north of Hartland Bay is marked by Bull Point lighthouse, which guides vessels navigating off the North Devon coast. It has a red sector light marking the Rockham Shoal and the Morte Stone off Morte Point. The light, established in 1879 on the headland near the village of Mortehoe, formed a triangle of lights together with Lundy and Hartland Point.

The idea for a light at Bull Point was first mooted in 1850 when a petition from clergy, shipowners, merchants and landowners was sent to the Trinity House Brethren asking for a lighthouse and stating that the 'barbarous conduct of lawless wreckers caused much loss of life and property'. In 1879, in response to these complaints, the lighthouse was built.

The original tower was 30ft in height from foundation to gallery, and stood 71ft from the cliff edge. The massive helical lantern added on top of the tower was 14ft in diameter and 14ft 6in high. The light was first shown on 12 August 1879, its beam was 154ft above sea level and it had a range of twenty nautical miles.

The other buildings that made up the station included a single-storey gable-ended building, 47ft by 28ft, in front of the tower, which contained the machinery for both the light and the fog horn, which had a range of up to four nautical miles.

The station was modernised in 1950, when it was connected to the mains water and two Lister diesel motors were installed to power the air compressor. In the keepers' quarters running hot and cold water was installed, together with flushing toilets.

The lighthouse gave good if unremarkable service until 18 September 1972, when the Principal Keeper noticed movement in the ground near the engine room and the passage

Bull Point

▶ The temporary light at Bull Point was in use from 1972 to 1976.

leading to the lighthouse, and saw two-inch fissures opening up. This was a prelude to events in the early hours of 24 September when 50ft of the cliff face fell into the sea and a further 50ft subsided, causing deep fissures to form inside the boundary wall. Walls cracked and the engine/fog signal station partly collapsed, leaving it in a perilous condition and putting the fog signal out of action.

A temporary measure was soon implemented to maintain the light. An old Trinity House light tower, which had been in use at Braunton Sands and subsequently given to the Nature Conservancy, was reacquired, moved to Bull Point, and the optic installed on top of it, an arrangement which was used for nearly four years. A hut was constructed for the three diaphone fog signals as a temporary measure.

In 1974 work began on a new lighthouse, built at a cost of £71,000. The new tower, 55ft tall and 180ft above mean high water, was designed and built so that the equipment from the old lighthouse, including the generator and fog signal house, could be utilised, albeit with modifications. Much of the equipment dates from 1960 when the station was electrified, while the optic, with a range of twenty-four miles, is now in its third site at Bull Point.

With the new lighthouse, the station was automated, and in 1988 the fog signal was discontinued. The keepers' houses were sold by Trinity House and are now used as holiday homes.

▼ The 1879 lighthouse and the compound with the keepers' houses, most of which was destroyed when the cliff collapsed.

▲ The 1975-built lighthouse is situated further up the cliff than the original tower, but some of the original service buildings remain.

◄ The functional lighthouse at Bull Point is situated about a mile north of the village of Mortehoe.

▼ Bull Point light seen from the sea.

67

Lundy

ESTABLISHED
1820

CURRENT TOWER
1897 (North and South)

AUTOMATED
1976

OPERATOR
Trinity House

ACCESS
Lundy Island is managed by the Landmark Trust and day visits by boat from Bideford, Ilfracombe or Clovelly are possible during the summer; the south light is accessible by a short climb up steps from the landing pier; the old light by a hike to the summit; the north light is a more than three miles over rough terrain from the landing pier

▶▶ Lundy North lighthouse was built in 1897 to a standard Trinity House design.

▶ Lundy North light commands spectacular views of the Bristol Channel, with the coasts of Wales and Devon visible on a clear day. The rail track leading from the station linked it to a landing stage cut into the rocks.

Lundy Island is three and a half miles long, three-quarters of a mile wide and lies in the Bristol Channel. In the eighteenth century hundreds of ships passed, and sometimes foundered, on this rocky outcrop. So in 1786 a syndicate of Bristol merchants started to erect a lighthouse on its summit, Chapel Hill. But their efforts came to nothing and it was not until 1820 that Trinity House had a lighthouse built by Joseph Nelson, and designed by Daniel Alexander.

The 96ft slightly-tapering granite tower was completed with a gallery and lantern and a window on the west side for a secondary light. The adjacent keepers' dwellings were also in granite and connected to the tower by a short corridor, and an additional keeper's cottage was nearby. The main light was originally a catoptric system giving a flashing white light visible for thirty-one miles, but this was later changed to a dioptric apparatus.

The problems with this light were that it revolved so quickly that at a distance it appeared fixed, and the fixed red light, which shone from the window in the tower, merged with it to form what appeared to be one beam. The idea was that the window shielded this light so it was only visible at four miles. Ships would steer clear until it was no longer visible, thus avoiding the island. The merging of the lights caused more harm than good, however, and the light was moved to the bottom of the tower, to no avail.

Another problem was fog, which obscured the light. To overcome this problem, a pair of fog cannons was installed on the western cliff, one of which, together with its associated buildings, is still in place. Trinity House continued to receive complaints regarding visibility, and so, in 1897 replaced the single light with two lights, one at each end of the island, lower down the cliff.

Lundy North lighthouse was constructed in a remote area on a plateau overlooking the Hen and Chickens. A landing stage was built at the base of the rocks

Lundy

▶▶ Lundy South lighthouse stands at the south-east corner of the island and its flashing white light is visible for fifteen miles.

▼ The old lighthouse on Lundy Island is situated in the middle of the island and was operational from 1819 to 1897. It is now used as a daymark and is open to visitors while the old keepers' cottages have been refurbished and can be rented by visitors.

with a cable stretched from the top of the cliff so that stores could be delivered via a traveller controlled from a winch housed at the top. A small railway ran the 100 yards to the lighthouse. Designed by Sir Thomas Matthews, the light was the most advanced in the world at the time. It consisted of a 56ft stone tower with split level single-storey keepers' dwellings and equipment rooms on each side.

The light was initially a petroleum vapour burner but was converted to electricity in 1971. It was automated and controlled from Lundy South in 1985. When modernised in 1991, it was converted to solar power and the optic in the lantern was removed. The light was mounted on the roof of the redundant fog signal building where a rotating beacon made by Orga produces a flashing white light visible for seventeen miles. The station was fully automated in 1994.

In order to build Lundy South lighthouse, an area of rock near the south-east corner of the island was levelled so that the light could be seen from all directions. The lighthouse was more compact than that in the north, with a 53ft circular stone tower attached to single-storey keepers' dwellings. The foghorn was mounted in a cylindrical tower on top of the lantern.

The majority of the equipment from the 1820 lighthouse was transferred here. The first light was a petroleum vapour burner, but was converted to electricity in 1971. When modernised in 1994, the station was automated and converted to solar power with the light in the lantern converted to an Orga rotating beacon.

Ilfracombe

ESTABLISHED
circa 1650

CURRENT TOWER
1819

OPERATOR
Trinity House

ACCESS
Via chapel on Lantern Hill

▶▶ Lantern Hill overlooks the small harbour at Ilfracombe.

▼ The chapel on Lantern Hill dates from about 1320, with the current light tower added by Trinity House in 1819. The original 1650 lantern can be seen at the right hand end of the building.

Ilfracombe boasts the largest harbour in North Devon, although much of it dries out at low tide. To the west of the entrance is a series of rocky outcrops and a conical land mass called Lantern Hill, upon which has been displayed for many centuries an aid to navigation.

In 1319 the stone-built slate-roofed chapel of St Nicholas ordered by Walter Stapleton, Bishop of Exeter, was constructed on its pinnacle. Although a primitive light may have been displayed, from about 1650 one was displayed on its western end to warn vessels of the rocks as they approached the harbour. In 1819 Trinity House took over this light, replaced it with a circular lantern on the roof, and twenty years later converted it to gas.

Mounted on the chapel's roof, the lantern is 37ft high with a focal plane of 130ft. The green light, which shows two flashes every five seconds, is now electrically powered and visible for six miles. Sometimes called Ilfracombe and sometimes Lantern Hill, it is claimed to be the oldest continuously exhibited light in the country.

The chapel has served many purposes during its time, being used as a refuge in the middle ages. In 1835 John Davie occupied it as lighthouse keeper and continued to do so with his wife and thirteen children until 1871, when vibration from the extensive harbour works made the chapel uninhabitable. It was later used for various purposes, such as a reading room, until after the Second World War when it fell into disrepair. It was restored by the Rotary Club in 1962 and is now open to visitors.

Other aids to navigation are located on the North and South Promenade Piers and the Inner Pier Head, with leading lights positioned in the south-east corner of the harbour.

Lynmouth Foreland

ESTABLISHED
1900

CURRENT TOWER
1900

AUTOMATED
1994

OPERATOR
Trinity House

ACCESS
Via the South West Coast Path from Countisbury, or a service road off A39

▶▶ Lynmouth Foreland lighthouse at Foreland Point, to the north-east of the small town of Lynmouth, faces north looking over the Bristol Channel.

▼ The old keepers' cottages are now managed by the National Trust.

The southern approaches to the Bristol Channel were marked by the lighthouses built at Hartland Point in 1874 and at Bull Point five years later. In 1900 Trinity House supplemented these two lights with a new lighthouse two miles east of the small town of Lynmouth at Foreland Point, and twenty miles east of Bull Point. Called Lynmouth Foreland, the station was constructed on a ledge two-thirds of the way down a 900ft cliff, with the unusual arrangement that the light was placed below the terrace of single-storey stone-built keepers' dwellings and service buildings.

The circular 49ft white tower, with gallery and lantern, originally housed an oil-powered light. In 1975, the station was electrified and a first order dioptric installed, giving a white flashing light visible for eighteen miles. An electric fog signal was built into the front of the tower.

Its remote location under the north-facing cliff means the station receives sunshine for just three months of the year, and so a special arrangement was applied whereby no keeper was assigned to the station for more than three years. This situation ceased in 1994, when the station was automated and the keepers were withdrawn. The cottages are now managed by the National Trust and available to let, but the tower is closed. The site can be reached via a cliff top walk along a path, which offers impressive views, which leads from the old inn near Countisbury.

The focal plane of the current optic is 67m above sea level. The optic itself is a first order dioptric apparatus, consisting of eight panels in two groups of four, revolving on a motor driven mercury float pedestal. The light character is four white flashes every fifteen seconds.

Watchet

ESTABLISHED
1862

CURRENT TOWER
1862

OPERATOR
Watchet Harbour Authority

ACCESS
The harbour piers are open to the public

▶▶ The red cast-iron light at the end of Watchet breakwater was built in 1862.

▼ The lighthouse on the end of the west breakwater is now is electrically powered.

The first mention of Watchet Harbour comes in the Anglo-Saxon chronicles, while by the mid-sixteenth century the harbour had a primitive jetty which was destroyed by a storm in 1659. By the early seventeenth century a stronger pier had been built to enable the export of wool and kelp to be undertaken.

The harbour was further developed in the nineteenth century, and in the 1860s two independent railways terminated at Watchet, bringing iron ore for export to Ebbw Vale, so the harbour was rebuilt with two stone breakwaters.

In 1862 the eye-catching lighthouse was built on the end of the new west breakwater by Hennet Spink & Else of Bridgwater at a cost of £75. It consists of a red 22ft hexagonal cast-iron tower supporting a white lantern complete with a green hexagonal roof. The lantern, with oil lamp, cost £90 and was supplied by Messrs Stevens & sons of London. It was erected with the assistance of Alfred Wedlake. The light is topped by an ornate weather vane and showed a fixed green light.

In 1900 the harbour was again damaged by storms and this resulted in Watchet Urban District Council taking over the running of the harbour and town from St Decuman's parish. The lighthouse was removed and subsequently re-erected on the new breakwater in 1905. The oil lamp was improved and a mechanism made by Chance Brothers installed to give an occulting green light every three seconds visible for nine miles.

On the end of the east breakwater is a single 9ft grey pole which carries two simple red lights displayed vertically with a range of three miles, and this was erected around 1900.

Burnham-on-Sea

ESTABLISHED
1801

CURRENT TOWER
1832

OPERATOR
Privately owned

ACCESS
The high light is to the north of the town in Berrow Road, and can be viewed from the road; the low light is on the beach half a mile north of the town

▶▶ The High Light at Burnham-on-Sea is now used as a private dwelling. An unusual feature was the spiral staircase, which did not reach the top, so the last two storeys had to be climbed by vertical ladders. A red day mark runs up the seaward side of the tower.

▶ (left) The 1801-built tower, which has been inactive since 1832, was originally four storeys tall.

▶ (right) An old postcard showing the High Light when in operation.

The lighthouses in Burnham-on-Sea had an unusual beginning when, around 1750, an old fisherman's wife living in a cottage close to the church put a candle in her window to help her husband find his way home. It saved his life and from then on the grateful sailors decided to pay her small sums of money to keep a candle burning.

Later, the sexton of the church gave the fisherman's wife five pounds for the rights to place a light on the church tower. Thus came about what is now known as Burnham-on-Sea Seafront Rear Range light. It is now shown as a fixed red light visible for three miles and is mounted on the 36ft tower of the Church of St Andrew, on the seafront. The tower has a slight lean due to subsidence. The Front Range is a simple light on a street lighting column on the promenade in front of the church.

In 1801 David Davis, the local curate, built a lighthouse, known locally as the Round Tower, which was attached to the verger's house at the north end of the churchyard. Originally a four-storey circular masonry tower, it showed a fire light through a window at the top. Because money raised locally was insufficient to maintain the light, a 100-year lease was granted to Davis in 1813, together with permission to collect dues from vessels entering the river Parrett.

The lease was bought out in 1829 by Trinity House, who decided to build a new lighthouse to the north and, upon its completion in 1932, the original light was deactivated. To avoid confusion, the top two levels of Davis' tower were removed and the top of the remainder castellated to avoid it being confused with the new light. It still stands behind the

Burnham-on-Sea

►► The Low Light at Burnham-on-Sea supported on wooden piles, with the High Light visible in the background left. There is a broad red day mark down the front of the tower.

▼ The Low Light, sometimes referred to as the 'lighthouse on legs', pictured during the early twentieth century, with the access steps at the back which have since been removed.

esplanade buildings just to the north of the Church of St Andrew.

In 1832 Joseph Nelson, working for Trinity House, built a new 99ft tower lighthouse to mark the channel into the river Parrett between Berrow Flats and Stert Flats, which became known locally as the Pillar Lighthouse. It originally had two chimneys and an elaborate weather vane, but these were later removed. Although some keepers' quarters were incorporated into the tower, cottages were also attached to it. The tower was coal fuelled and the fixed white light paraffin fuelled, and the old paraffin fuel store still exists in the rear gardens. The light was displayed through a window and half gallery near the top and was visible for seventeen miles.

In 1922 it became the first light in the UK to be automated, and the keepers' cottages were sold. The light was extinguished in 1993 and the lighthouse itself was sold. A Grade II listed building, it is now a holiday let with the ladders replaced by stairs and the 6th floor removed.

When the high light was commissioned it was found that too low a vantage point had been selected to account for the rise and fall of the tide, so Joseph Nelson built a Low Light later in 1832. This 36ft tall, 15ft square close-boarded wooden tower with a conical roof supported on nine wooden pile legs is situated on the beach 800 yards in front of the High Light.

Initially the paraffin light showed a white flash every 7.5 seconds, with a separate directional light, through a window near the top. The light was deactivated 1969, but was reactivated in 1993. At this time the electric main light displayed a white flash every 7.5 seconds with a range of twelve miles. The directional light was shown through a window lower down.

Blacknore Point

ESTABLISHED
1894

CURRENT TOWER
1894

OPERATOR
Trinity House

DEACTIVATED
2010

ACCESS
Via the coast path from Portishead; or by private footpath from Nore Road

▶▶ The 36ft hexagonal tower at Blacknore on the upper Bristol Channel, built to help shipping using the river Avon, was deactivated in 2010.

▼ An old image of the lighthouse and the nearby Nautical School, which closed in 1982.

When the lighthouse at Blacknore Point, just south of Portishead, was built in 1894 by Trinity House to guide ships into the Avon, it was the only light in the area. As a consequence it was often referred to as Portishead lighthouse and care has to be taken not to confuse it with the lighthouse built later at Portishead Point.

It is one of a number of prefabricated lights and consists of a white 36ft hexagonal cast-iron tower on a six-legged cast-iron lattice frame, mounted on a simple plinth with a lantern and gallery. The flashing white light was initially powered by mains gas stored in its own gas storage tank, fed from the village mains, with enough for two nights so that disruption to the local supply would not affect operations.

The owners of Black Nore farm used to visit the light twice a day to light and extinguish the light. They also wound the mechanism which used weights to keep the optical system revolving. It was automated and converted to electricity in 1941 using a fourth order Catadioptric Biform 4 panel lens floating on a bed of mercury. This gave two flashes every twenty seconds with a range of fifteen miles. So that the light could be quickly extinguished during the war, a switch was installed in the farm.

The original mechanical lens rotating mechanism remained in place until 1970, when it was replaced by an electric motor. The fourth order biform dioptric and 100-watt lamp showed a white group flashing light twice every ten seconds, with a range of fifteen miles. After an appraisal of navigation requirements by Trinity House, it was decommissioned on 27 September 2010 and in October 2011 was sold to a trust for preservation at a cost of £1.

Nautical School and Black Nose Point Lighthouse, Portishead

Portishead Point

ESTABLISHED
1930

CURRENT TOWER
1930

OPERATOR
Bristol Port Company

ACCESS
Via the esplanade at Portishead

▶▶ Portishead Point light is more usually known as Battery Point, the name of the land on which it stands.

▼ The tower, built by Chance Brothers of Smethwick, stands 30ft high and the light has a range of sixteen miles.

Portishead Point and Battery Point adjoin each other and when this light on Portishead Point was built in 1930 by the Bristol Port Company, it quickly became referred to locally as Battery Point Light. This avoided confusion with Blacknore Point light a mile to the south west which, ironically, had become known locally as Portishead light.

The tower, built by Chance Brothers, is of an unusual design consisting of a black 30ft high lattice tower on a white Ferro concrete base. The light was activated by March 1931. The control equipment is housed in two black metal enclosed areas, one at the base of the tower and one at the top. There is a narrow walkway on concrete supports connecting it to the shore.

The group flashing white light, which gives three quick flashes every ten seconds and is visible for sixteen miles, is provided by a simple lens mounted on top. The original sixth order Chance Brothers flashing beacon was initially powered via an electrical circuit direct from Portishead Power Station, but the light is now powered by batteries recharged from a mains supply. In 2004 the light was replaced and by 2005 an auxiliary light had also been added. The solar panels are a recent addition.

A large fog bell weighing two tons was suspended on an iron frame mounted on the concrete base when the tower was first built, but because of concerns about the strength of the whole structure it was removed on 25 July 1998 and replaced by a fog horn giving one blast every twenty seconds. The bell has recently been located and there are moves afoot to display it in the town.

Avonmouth

ESTABLISHED
1839

CURRENT TOWER
1908

OPERATOR
Bristol Port Company

ACCESS
Avonmouth Docks is a restricted area; various vantage points on Avonmouth waterfront offer views of the lights

▶▶ The North Pierhead Light at Avonmouth Docks was built in 1908.

▼ The 30ft South Pierhead Light, nearest camera, is one of two lights marking the entrance to Avonmouth Docks.

Trinity House built the first light at Avonmouth in 1839. Situated where Avonmouth Docks are today, it consisted of a white 65ft castellated octagonal brick tower with two six-roomed keepers' cottages attached by short corridors. The light was visible for fourteen miles and marked the entrance of the river Avon where it met the Bristol Channel. The structure was demolished in 1902 when work started on the new docks.

The much larger dock complex, based around the Royal Edward Dock, was opened in 1908. During the construction work, a light was displayed on a wooden structure as a temporary measure until 1908, by which time a pair of lighthouses had been constructed on the completed dock piers. These new lighthouses, called Avonmouth Docks North Pier Head and Avonmouth Docks South Pier Head, were both ornate circular structures built of Norwegian granite. The slightly tapered towers have solid doorways and windows and the lights are housed in white circular lanterns with domed roofs and white railings round the galleries.

The lights were operated by Trinity House initially, then the Port of Bristol Authority took them over, and, since 1991, the Bristol Port Company has been responsible for them. Situated in Royal King Edward Docks, the South Pier Light, completed in 1907, shows an occulting electric light visible for ten miles, with red and green sectors. The North Pier Light, which is 52ft tall, was completed in 1908. Its flashing white electrical light is visible for eighteen miles.

River Severn

ESTABLISHED
Various dates, from 1886

CURRENT TOWERS
Between 1937 and 2011

AUTOMATED
1948 onwards

OPERATOR
Gloucester Harbour Trustees

ACCESS
Via a path along the river bank, from which the lights can be seen

▼ Chapel Rock light is situated off Beachley Point near the ruins of an old chapel, downstream from the old Severn Bridge. The light shown here was replaced by a slim lattice tower supporting a white light flashing every 2.6 seconds in June 2010.

The approach to Gloucester Docks via the river Severn requires careful navigation, particularly through the Shoots between the motorway bridges. The river's aids to navigation, administered by Gloucester Harbour Trustees, mark where the river is crossed by the M4 bridge to Sharpness Docks; from there up to Gloucester are no land-based aids to navigation. The lights at Shoots, Charston Rock and Redcliffe are in Wales. The first lights are on the western side of the river as far as Pillhouse Rocks, after which they are all on the eastern side.

Bulwark • Situated near the river Wye entrance, the light at Bulwark was established in June 1966 to operate on conjunction with the blue light on the centre span of the Wye motorway bridge to form a lead into the river. When Chepstow was declared a daylight port only in September 1982, this light was discontinued.

Today, there is a yellow locker with a red H-section post upon which are the remains of a gas operated lantern and sun valve.

Chapel Rock • The light on Chapel Rock, just off Beachley Point, was first erected on a wooden structure in 1886. It had an oil-fired fixed white light with green sectors on each side to guide vessels clear of the rocks as the Wye and Severn channels diverged. In 1907 the wooden structure was replaced by a black lattice steel tower. The light was converted to battery operation in 1947 and, to save battery life, flashing operation. It was converted to acetylene in 1951 and to mains electricity in 1983. In 2010 it was replaced by a 20ft lattice tower showing a flashing white light every 2.5 seconds.

Lyde Rock • Erected in 1896 on an iron-framed structure, the oil-powered light on Lyde Rock, with a fixed white light

◀ Berkley Pill Front Range was refurbished in 2008 using the lantern from Sheperdine Front Range.

▼ Berkley Pill Rear Range was refurbished in July 2010 using the refurbished lantern from the Front Range.

and red sectors, guided vessels past the Hen and Chickens Rock. Following a ship collision in 1941, the iron tower was replaced by a 40ft steel lattice tower. In 1947 a battery-operated light was installed and, to improve battery life, it was converted to flashing. Battery life remained a problem, so in 1951 the light was converted to acetylene gas. In 1983 the original lantern was removed, and the light was housed in a lantern, having been converted to mains electricity. Initially quick flashing white and red, it was changed to quick red with a range of five miles in 2007.

Slime Road Leading Lights

• Established on wooden structures in 1915, the two fixed white lights were intended to guide vessels along the Slime Road channel. They were replaced in 1941 by a Front Range light housed in a white steel nut built into the hillside, where a white stripe is painted into the cliff face. The Rear Range

River Severn

consisted of a tall black lattice steel tower, which supports a white circular lantern and gallery. The oil power was replaced by batteries in 1948, with the lights converted to flashing. They were synchronised in 1953 and converted to mains electricity in 1963, at which point fixed yellow fluorescent tubes were installed. This was changed to blue in 1981.

Sedbury • To mark the channel under the motorway bridge from Lyde Rock into Slime Road Channel, a light was established by the road contractors in 1962.

Initially two mains-powered vertical fixed blue fluorescent tubes were mounted on a wooden pole; this was replaced by two vertical fixed red lights on a 33ft abacus mast in 1988.

Inward Rocks • Situated at Pillhouse Rocks, these leading lights provide passage into the Barnacle Channel. They were established in 1886 with fixed white oil-burning lights on timber structures. The Front Range was replaced by a steel lattice tower in 1907, converted to mains electricity in 1962 and replaced by a circular fibreglass housing in 1985. The Rear Range was replaced by a steel mast in 1961, electrified in 1962 and in 1985 replaced by an Abacas mast which shows a fixed white light.

Narwood Beacons with Counts and Ledges Buoys • As the channel veers west, the major obstacles are Narwood, Count and Winstone rocks followed by The Ledges. It is likely the first aid to navigational on the river was a beacon on Winstone Rock, with a later beacon on Counts Rock. The remains of these beacons still exist, although they have been superseded by Counts and Ledges light buoys. Narwood Beacons were established in 1900 with oil-burning fixed white lights on timber poles. The lights were changed to gas-powered flashing white lights in 1926. In 1964 both lights were replaced by steel poles, the front 39ft in height and the rear 56ft. In 1987 they were converted to solar.

▼ The metal radar structure erected at Sheperdine as the Front Range in 1996 replaced a steel lattice tower of a design similar to the Rear Range, which is shown on page 91.

In May 2011 the Counts Buoy was replaced by a 40ft lattice tower painted yellow at its lower section and black above. It carries a top mark and exhibits a quick flashing white light visible for two miles.

Sheperdine • Established in 1888 to mark the eastern end of the Barnacle channel, Sheperdine's oil-powered white leading lights were initially supported on wooden poles. The poles were replaced by 39ft black lattice steel towers in 1906, and in 1948 the lights were converted to battery power. They were synchronised in 1953 and in 1961 converted to fixed white. The Rear Range, which initially carried a fog bell, was changed to a single monopole mast carrying vertical fluorescent lights and a red and white daymark in 2010. The Front Range was changed to a 25ft square grey enclosure with eight vertical fluorescent lights and a radar antenna mounted on a gallery supported by a circular steel tube in 1996.

Hills Flats buoy • Hills Flats rock was marked with an unlit buoy in 1899. In 1961 this was replaced by a green can buoy fitted with gas lighting, manufactured by Charles Hill of Bristol. It was converted to solar power and battery operation in 1987. A lantern utilising modern light emitting diode technology was installed in September 2000, together with a solid-state voltage regulator. In May 2011 the buoy was replaced by a 40ft lattice tower painted green, with a green conical topmark. It exhibits a flashing green light which is visible for two miles.

Fishing House • A single fixed white light, with a red sector to mark Haywards Rock, was established in 1886 on a wooden pole. In 1894 a pair of

▲ The steel tower at Sheperdine Rear Range supported a fog bell, which was installed in 1961. The bell has since been discontinued and is now displayed on a warehouse in Gloucester docks. The tower shown here was replaced by an Abacus column in 2010.

◄ The fibreglass structure at Fishinghouse Front Range was installed in 1985.

River Severn

▲ When Sheperdine Front Range was replaced in 1996, the lantern was refurbished and installed at Berkley Pill Front Range in 2008. The lantern pictured here is the refurbished original Berkley Pill Front Range which was ready to be installed on the Rear Range in July 2010.

fixed white leading lights was installed on wooden structures, marking a line through Bull Rock Channel, with the red sector incorporated into the Front Range. The lights were converted to battery power in 1948, and flashing in character; they were synchronised in 1953. In 1960 the Front Range was replaced by a steel lattice tower and the timber in the Rear Range renewed. The lights were converted to mains power, using four fluorescent tubes at each location. In 1985 they were again renewed, with the Rear Range made up by four vertical white fluorescent tubes mounted on a 39ft Abacus mast. The Front Range is shown from a 13ft glass fibre conical tower, with four white fluorescent tubes on top, with a red sector, and an orange and white daymark.

Haywards Rock Beacon • In 1906 an unlit buoy was placed adjacent to Haywards Rock. It was replaced by a small winker beacon in 1956 and by a gas lit steel buoy in 1958. This was altered to solar power in 1987 and replaced by a plastic buoy in 1991. Due to high maintenance costs, it was replaced by a 40ft steel beacon showing a quick flashing white light, which was mounted on the rock in 1999.

Conigre Leading Lights •
To delineate the Low Way channel across Lydney Sand, a pair of oil-powered fixed white lights on wooden poles were commissioned in 1891. In 1898 a green and red sector was added to mark Bull Rock. The character was changed to white flashing in 1948, when the lights were converted to battery power, and they were synchronised in 1953. When Berkeley Nuclear Power Station was constructed in 1960, the poles were replaced by steel lattice towers. The Rear Range is 96ft high and the Front Range 63ft, both supporting vertically-disposed fluorescent tubes.

Bull Beacon • One of a number of small aids to navigation on the river Severn, Bull Beacon was established in 1894 to mark the starboard side of the channel.

◀ Bull Beacon is one of a number of small aids to navigation on the river Severn. The tower shown was erected in August 2005.

It was charged in 1958 to a chain stayed gas beacon. It was demolished by a vessel in 1984, being replaced by a 50ft steel mast in 1988. In 2002 it was converted to solar power with an LED lantern. The tower shown was erected in August 2005 .

Berkeley Pill • In 1906 a pair of fixed oil lights transferred from Sheperdine was erected on wood poles to mark the channel into Sharpness docks. In 1926 they were changed to gas powered. In 1937 the current black lattice steel towers were erected, each with a white steel circular lantern and platform. The Rear Range was 40ft and the Front Range 34ft. In 1951 the gas system was replaced by battery-powered lights, which flashed white and were synchronised in 1953. In 1964 they were converted to mains electricity.

Panthurst • Although posts were erected at Panthurst in 1894, it was not until 1912 that a light was shown. It consisted of a single lit beacon showing a fixed-white oil-powered light screened on each side to indicate guide vessels into Sharpness docks. In 1974 two mains-powered blue fluorescent tubes, in the form of a cross, were installed, and then, in 1987, following improvements to the flood bank, another light was installed which remains in use. It consists of a single vertical mains-powered blue fluorescent tube mounted on a 15ft circular yellow glass-fibre column.

Sharpness • A wooden lighthouse showing a fixed red light was established prior to 1893 which, when aligned with a light on the North Pier, provided a lead to the west of Black Rock. When the Bull Rock was levelled in 1984, a new channel was established so the light was discontinued and demolished. Today, a series of small lights on poles mark the harbour entrance.

Glossary

▲ Lizard.

▲ Lundy Old light.

▲ Crow Point.

Acetylene A highly combustible gas which burns with an intensely bright flame.

Argand lamps A bright and relatively clean-burning lamp invented by Francois-Pierre Ami Argand in 1783.

Automated An unmanned light controlled externally; all the major UK lighthouses are automated with Trinity House controlling and monitoring its lights from the Corporation's Depot in Harwich.

Beacon A structure, usually land based, either lit or unlit, used to guide mariners.

Characteristic The identifying feature of a lighthouse is its characteristic; for example the light could be described as fixed, or flashing.

Daymark Light towers often also serve as daymarks, landmarks that are visible from the sea during daylight acting as aids to navigation.

Dioptric lens A development by Augustin Fresnel consisting of a bull's eye lens surrounded by a series of concentric glass prisms. Dioptric lenses were classified by their focal length.

Elevation The elevation refers to a light's height above sea level; the higher the elevation, the greater the range.

Flashing light A light where the period of light is less than the period of darkness.

Fog signals A sound signal used to warn mariners in times of fog or heavy weather.

Gallery A walkway beneath the lantern room to enable access for maintenance.

High light The taller or higher of a pair of lights.

Isophase light A light where the periods of light and dark are equal.

Keepers The persons responsible for maintaining and keeping the light at an aid to navigation, including the associated buildings.

Lanby The abbreviated term for Large Automatic Navigation Buoy, a modern floating unmanned aid to navigation often used in place of a lightship.

Lanterns The glass-enclosed space at the top of a lighthouse housing the lens or optic; lanterns are often encircled by a narrow walkway called the gallery.

Lightship A vessel powered or unpowered designed to support a navigational aid.

Low light The shorter or lower of the two lights used to mark a channel or hazard.

Occulting Where the period a light exhibited is greater than its period of eclipse; this can be achieved in several ways.

Range lights Lights displayed in pairs which are used to mark a navigable channel.

Reflector A system which intensifies light by reflecting the light source into a beam, both to increase intensity and to enable the beam to be manipulated to produce differing light characteristics.

Training wall A bank or wall erected below water level in a river or harbour mouth to train the water flow.

Appendix

Bibliography

Boyle, Martin: various books covering individual lighthouses (1996-98).

Hague, Douglas B. and Christie, Rosemary: Lighthouses: Their Architecture, History and Archaeology (Gomer Press, Dyfed, 1975).

Hardy, W. J.: Lighthouses: Their history and romance (Fleming H. Revell Co, London, 1895).

Nicholson, Christopher: Rock Lighthouses of Britain (Patrick Stephens, Somerset, 1995).

Tarrant, Michael: Cornwall's Lighthouse Heritage (Twelveheads Press, Truro, 1st edition 1990).

Woodman, Richard and Wilson, Jane: The Lighthouses of Trinity House (Thomas Reed Publications, 2002).

Websites

www.alk.org.uk Association of Lighthouse Keepers; archive, museum, quarterly journal.

www.lighthousedepot.com Comprehensive list of world lights with details, photos, locations and links.

www.trabas.de/enindex.html List of world lights including minor lights with photos.

www.unc.edu/~rowlett/lighthouse/index.htm Comprehensive list of world lights with photos and links.

www.trinityhouse.co.uk Trinity House website with details of all their lighthouses.

www.michaelmillichamp.ukgateway.net England and Wales operational and non-operational lights.

www.gloucesterharbourtrustees.org.uk/history River Severn lights and beacons.

▲ Lynmouth Foreland.

Acknowledgements

Many people have assisted with this book and we are grateful to them all: Vikki Gilson and John Chapel at Trinity House; Mike Johnson, Harbour Master at Gloucester Harbour Trustees; Nicola Saunders, Lundy Warden; and Gerry Douglas-Sherwood.

We gratefully acknowledge the people who have supplied images for possible inclusion. All photographs are by Nicholas Leach, except Association of Lighthouse Keepers 7, 9; John Mobbs 8, 10, 11 (lower), 18, 22, 40, 42, 44, 46, 52, 54, 56 (lower), 60, 66, 80, 82; Trinity House 11 (upper), 12 (lower), 36 (lower), 41; Paul Richards 12 (upper), 16, 17, 27, 28, 29, 36 (upper), 38, 39, 43, 47, 50, 51, 56 (upper); Phil Weeks 20, 45; John Chappell 21, 35, 95 (lower); Tim Stevens 31, 33, 37; David Wilkinson 58, 95 (top); Tony Denton 63, 89, 90, 91, 92, 93; and Michel Forand 64.

Finally, our gratitude extends to Maureen and Sarah for their support and patience during the preparation of this book.

▲ St Anthony's Head.

▲ Godrevy.

Index

Argand Lamp 20, 24, 26, 30, 46
Abacus Mast 90, 92
Avon, river 82, 86
Avonmouth 86
Banjo Pier 14
Barnacle Channel 90
Basset, Francis 51
Battery Point Light 84
Bayly, Captain Simon 42
Berkeley Pill 93
Berkley Nuclear Power Station 92
Berrow Flats 80
Bishop Rock 9, 42, 44
Blacknore Point 82, 84
Boscawen Point 28
Braunton 60, 62, 66
Bristol Channel 4, 13, 54, 58, 68, 84, 86
Bristol Port Company 84, 86
Bull Beacon 92, 93
Bull Point 9, 64, 66, 74
Bulwark 88
Burnham-on-Sea 6, 78, 80
Camel, river 54
Carkeek, Arthur 46
Carn Bass Rock 30
Casquets 22
Chance Brothers 32, 46, 76, 84
Chapel Rock 88
Christie Estate Trust 62
Clayton, Sir John 42
Conigre 92
Counts Buoy 90
Crisp, Michael H. 28
Crow Point 60, 62, 94
Davie, John 72
Davies, Rev David 6, 78
Douglass, Sir James 32, 40, 44, 48
Duke of Gloucester, HRH 28
Ebbw Vale 76
Eddystone 10, 34, 44
Elkins, Thomas 40
Falmouth 20, 22, 26
Fishing House 91, 92
Fonnereau, Thomas 8, 22
Fowey 4, 10, 14, 16, 18
Fresnel Lens 20, 24
Gear Rock 26
Gloucester Docks 88
Gloucester Harbour Trustees 88
Godrevy 1, 9, 10, 52, 95
Gribben Head 12, 18
Gulf Rock 51
Gumards Head 46
Gwenapp Head 28, 36
Hartland Point 9, 58, 64, 74

Harvey, Edward 48
Harvey, James 48
Hayle 46, 50
Haywards Rock Beacon 92
Heritage Lottery Fund 24
Hill, Captain Hugh 42
Hill, Charles of Bristol 91
Hills Flats 91
Hood vapour burner 32, 56
Horse Rock 51
Hugh Town 38
Humphries 28
Ilfracombe 5, 72
Instow 62
Inward Rocks 90
Killigrew, Sir John 7, 22
Lantern Hill 72
Ledges Buoy 90, 91
Leland, John 48
Lepaute, Henry 54
Limmicks 14
Lizard 4, 6, 7, 8, 22, 24, 94
Lizard Heritage Centre 24
Longships 4, 9, 30, 32, 46, 54
Looe 14, 18
Lundy 54, 58, 64, 68, 70, 94
Lyde Rock 88, 89
Lydney Sand 92
Lynmouth Foreland 74, 95
Manacles 20
Matthews, John 24, 32
Matthews, Sir Thomas 46, 70
Mevagissey 4, 10, 18
Mounts Bay 27
Narlwood Beacon 90
Nautophone 20, 27
Needles 14
Nelson, Joseph 60, 68, 80
Newlyn 11, 27
Olver, Jacob and Thomas (Falmouth) 20, 54
Ordnance Survey datum 27
Panthurst 93
Parish, Richard 22
Parrett, river 78, 80
Pendeen 12, 46
Peninnis 9, 38, 42
Penpol Creek 50
Penzance 4, 5, 10, 26, 34
Pharos (Alexandra) 4, 5
Pillhouse Rocks 88, 90
Polperro 15
Port of Bristol Authority 84, 86
Portishead Point 82, 84
Portishead Power Station 84
Portreath 51

Raymond, The 26
Rosemodress Cliffs 28
Round Island 3, 9, 40
Royal Edward Dock 86
Runnelstone Rocks 28, 32, 36
Sandy & Co. 26
Sennen Cove 11, 46
Severn, river 88, 89, 90, 91, 92, 93
Sharpness 93
Sheperdine 91
Slime Road 89, 90
Smalls 44
Smeaton, John 30, 34, 48, 58
Smith, Henry 30, 34
Sperm Oil 26
Spink, Henry and Else 76
Spy House Point 15
St Agnes 7, 8, 22, 38, 42, 44
St Andrew church 78
St Anthony's 10, 20, 95
St Catherine's Chapel 16
St Catherine's Point 16
St Duceman's Parish 76
St Ives 10, 46, 48, 52
St Martin's Head 40
St Mary's 38, 42
St May's Sound 38
St Micheal's Mount 5
Stapleton, Walter 72
Stert Flatts 80
Stevens and Sons 76
Stothert and Pitt 48
Stuckley, Lady 58
Supertyphon fog horn 56
Sutcliffe, James 52
Tater Du 10, 28
Tawe, river 60, 62
Temple, Frederick 58
Three Stone Oar 46
Tideland lantern 56
Trevithick Trust 24
Trevose Head 9, 46, 54, 56
Trinity House 4, 6, 8, 9, 10, 20, 22, 24, 28, 30, 32, 34, 36, 40, 42, 52, 54, 58, 62, 64, 66, 68, 72, 74, 78, 82, 86
Walker, James 20, 34, 44, 52
Watchet 76
Wedlake, Alfred 76
Whiston, William 38
Whitehouse Point 14, 17
Wilkins, H. and Sons 54
Winstone Rock 90
Wolf Rock 4, 9, 11, 30, 34, 36
Wyatt, Samuel 30
Wye, river 88